THIS IS FINE

THIS IS FINE

#WOKE

poems, 2011–2017
santino j. rivera

broken sword publications
saint augustine, fla

BPS

Broken Sword Publications
Saint Augustine, Florida, USA

First Printing November 2017
Printed in the US of Fuckin' A

Artwork & design by Emilio Medina of muyCreative
muycreative.com
Special thanks to Lisa Rivera for proofreading.

Broken Sword Publications, LLC
Web: brokenswordpublications.com
Store: bsp.bigcartel.com
E-Mail: mail@brokenswordpublications.com
Twitter: @brokenswordpub
IG: @BrokenSwordPublications
Facebook: Broken Sword Publications

ISBN 978-0-9896313-3-4

CONTENTS

ONE

I am not a taco
it's not a victory
chicano poets
chicano soul
the chicano get down

TWO

end of the line
a poem for llewelyn
goddess of death
death is a mujer, part 4
the last love letter
.38 special and a bottle of olde e

THREE

no colored allowed
an outrage
a poem about gated communities & the children who walk through
them
a poem about gun rights in ameriKKKa
hashtag blow me
¡gentrify this!
come to heaven (it's whiter here!)
the st. augustine movement, 1964: a poem
there's no such thing as reverse racism!
never forget

the ballad of troy davis
the 13th amendment
stand your ground

FOUR

you can't hear bob seger
the worst televeision show of all-time
this is what we do now
howl (with apologies to a. ginsberg)
kill yourselfie
the independence day that never comes
hashtag buy stuff, hashtag shut the fuck up and die
2015
librarian's creed
the vultures of hotel florida
what does the billboard say?
the end is nigh (and ode to political season)
fuck me for your service
bad news is the new heroin, so shoot up, buttercup
targeted killing in the age of hope and change
merchandise no. 5
drone on the range
this is some gourmet shit!
the in-house drive-by strikes back
blue pills
knives and guns and gang fights in the age of hope and change
amnesia is fun

nobody's listening
nothing to see here
perception is reality
pissing contest
are you ready for some football?!
killing the messenger
once upon a time
only here
we win yet?
after the internet
side effects of drugs advertised on tv
DNC 2016 opening speech

FIVE

more demons
don't answer the goddamn phone!
gawd
what the 90s were like
21 years ago
circles
phone calls from ghosts
mind's eye
latchkey kids and jehovah's amazing technicolor dream park
the best years of your life!
the joneses
one day you're raising hell
errand boys and grocery clerks

tradition

acoma street

fear and lothing in public spaces

half-remembered dreams

run

the grass

2017

Even the apocalypse didn't stop us from killing one another over ideology.

- Artyom Alekseyevich Chyornyj

INTRO

I hate poetry. There, I said it. Yep, you read that right and no, I'm not joking. I realize how that sounds, here in a book of poetry (my third), but it's true – I hate the stuff. Okay, maybe that's not completely accurate...I *loathe* poetry and poets.

Poets are the lepers of the literary world. They are the beaten and neglected step-children of the written word. You can walk into almost any bookstore in the world and if they even have a poetry section you can bet your sweet ass it'll be tiny. And what's on it usually? The classics, with maybe a smattering of the modern stuff. Why? Because poets suck and everyone hates them.

If Rodney Dangerfield were still alive even he would get more respect than most poets. If someone asked what 100 poets on the bottom of the sea floor was, the overwhelming response would be: a good start. Save the lawyers, kill the poets, that's most people's motto.

No one likes poets. No one reads poetry. No one talks to poets and absolutely no one respects poets. Most folks pretend that poets don't even exist. Alas, we do.

Contrary to popular belief, poetry is an affliction, not a talent. Once you are cursed with it there is no turning back – you're fucked.

I tried to quit poetry many times over the course of the past couple of decades, but it never took. I always found myself like some goddamned junkie, right back at it, with a pen in my arm, stringing together nonsense to satisfy some wicked and primal urge, chasing that original high.

And that original high? All poets will know what I'm talking about. It happens when you read your stuff in public and it elicits a strong and positive reaction from the audience. People applaud – they hoot, holler and cheer and you're standing there like some asshole, completely dumbfounded that people actually got your message. It's hypnotic. It's also addictive.

I got hooked years ago, in some long-gone coffee shop in pre-gentrified Denver, and spent the next 20 years chasing that high; but just like crack, it's never as good as the first time.

i

So why do it, you ask? It's not like there was ever a choice. Let me rewind a little bit.

I wasn't born a poet. Unlike many haughty, pompous and award-crusted poets with accolades up their ass, I didn't write my first poem until I found myself, by accident, in a college classroom. I was never destined for college – I only ended up there because my dream of being a musician fell through.

I was not and never will be an academic. Truth be told, I was a fuckup with a chip on his shoulder who found himself in college surrounded by kids who didn't look like me who had prepared themselves for academia all their lives. Me? I'd prepared to be a rock and roll gangster. Ha!

So, it was purely an accident that I found myself in a creative writing class that I didn't *really* belong in. We were told to write poetry – no rules, no expectations – and I'll be goddamned: I liked it. And not only did I like it but my peers liked it too, as did my professors.

Hell, I didn't even know I could write and yet here I was, getting praise from eggheads and literary types – me, this lanky, angry Chicano kid who never got above a C in high school, and who would have probably beat the hell out of most of these nerds given half the chance.

And for this reason I do not relate to most, if any, of my contemporaries. I'm not cut from the same cloth as they are. Most of these Pulitzer-focused and self-pretentious folks were groomed for this shit while I was getting high and cruising a lowrider down Federal Boulevard. I do not mean to make it sound like I'm better than these people, just that while they were in AP classes in high school, I was ditching class and killing brain cells.

Still, I'd found a calling. And true to my "don't tell me what to do, Jack" attitude, I reveled in the freedom of it all. I discovered the *high* of sharing my writing with strangers and watching it affect them. To me, it wasn't much different than playing on stage with my guitar. I was hooked.

Soon after, I started discovering the rule breakers in the poetry and literary world and I fell even harder. I never cared for most of the classics and the modern poetry world made me want to retch. No, I found myself digging people like William S. Burroughs, Hunter Thompson and Henry Rollins, and of all things: lyrics to songs.

Suddenly, it became clear to me that poetry could be *anything* and that there were no rules. I dug that – still do.

The funny thing is that no one considers song lyrics poetry – song lyrics are *cool*. Musicians are cool. Poetry, in the immortal worlds of detective David Mills, is for *faggots*.

But I'd be lying to you if I said that I ever called myself a poet. I never have and once I left the academic world behind I soon discovered just how lowly poets are. And so I called myself a writer instead, trying to mask the fact that I wrote poetry – trying desperately to be cool. I tried to write like Rollins and Burroughs and styled my work as "hardcore."

I called myself a journalist. I called myself an author. I called myself a publisher. All of these things were true – I was! But I was ashamed to call myself a poet.

No longer.

Hello, my name is Santino and I am a poet. This is my poetry and detective Mills can go fuck himself.

You are probably here because you're familiar with my work. Or maybe you're not and this is your first introduction to it. Either way, I've never been overly proud or boastful of my own work because I've always ran from the "poet" label, trying my best to convince people that what they were reading was anything but poetry.

I can tell you in no uncertain terms that I am proud of this book. I think it's probably my best work to date, but I am biased.

My first instinct with this book was to let it stand on its own, with no explanation. But I soon realized that due to the nature of how it was written and the span of time that it covers that it was impossible to *not* explain it.

I wrote much of this book online. During the early part of this period, I used *Tumblr* (a social media platform), as a digital journal of sorts, for rough drafts and ideas. Years before this process I would use pen and paper journals for this purpose but I enjoyed the Tumblr format because it allowed me to edit things endlessly and share them if I wished to do so.

I started penning poem after poem as drafts there. Some of them I would share and publish on my Tumblr and others I would keep to myself. And for a while it was good but I started to notice something about sharing things on social media and that was that it was all so utterly disposable. This is problematic for several reasons.

Once I published something on Tumblr it was relevant for maybe 24-hours. After that it was flushed and forgotten down the digital toilet, never to be heard from again. This grew tiresome for things I believed deserved permanence. This was, after all, my work.

It wasn't all bad. Sometimes, things received some traction and they stayed afloat for quite a while – that's the nature of social media – if you're popular your words gain a little notoriety for a time. This can also be a double-edged sword but I digress.

I had one poem in particular, which is in this book, gain so much attention that it made me "Tumblr famous," which is to say that the poem itself gained extreme popularity (by Tumblr standards) and was shared hundreds of thousands of times, if not more.

It eventually lost all attribution to me and was borrowed from, stolen and eventually it died. My presence on Tumblr also died.

Tumblr, for all intents and purposes, was invaded by lunatics and zealots. It became a platform for the hysterical and the unhinged. I fled shortly after the invasion and much of this book is a reaction to that. If nothing else this book is a printed version of me standing outside, shaking my fist, and shouting at the top of my lungs for all the kids to get the fuck off.

We live in bizarre times, which is an understatement. Things happen so fast now and are forgotten almost immediately. Nothing has any permanence online. Can you remember what you were upset about last month? Last year? 5 years ago? Right.

And that's where the permanence of writing comes in. This is where I believe in the superiority of the printed word over the written one. This is where books have the edge over social media blogs.

I have to apologize for the format of this book –
These poems are not in chronological order. I wish I had the discipline to date them when I write but I do not and for that I am sorry. I have tried to organize these works in a way that keeps their subject matter close together, though there are lapses. Sometimes books fit together in a way that only makes sense to the book – this is one of those times.

Most of what you are reading in this book was written in the heat of the moment. It was written with passion and fury and a dark sense of humor – I pulled no punches. I wrote this stuff fully intending to light some fires. I took moments that were important to me and sculpted them into little works of art.

Not all of them are "good" in my opinion and I cut a great deal of fat from this book, despite its size. Still, this is about as naked and raw as it gets, but I know no other way to write.

I imagine some of the works in this book will anger people. Some will cause people to turn their backs. I am okay with that. This has already happened online because I dare to have an opinion. I am a free speech absolutist and for my sin I am a heretic. So be it.

This book took a long time to finish – too long. And the longer I hesitated the more irrelevant some of the pieces became. I began to buy into the hysteria online and the push to self-censor and to not offend. I started to question if I should publish this book at all...and then I woke the fuck up and reminded myself who I am and why I write/publish.

Fuck your feelings. This book is for me. Much of this work is personal. This is me on the page.

One of the things I find most interesting about my work is that it tends to draw people who either don't like poetry or who have never read poetry. One of the comments I've heard more than a few times is: *I didn't know poetry could be like this!*

I take great pride in writing that kind of material because as I said, I'm not like those other poets, but you already know that if you're reading this.

That said, this may or may not be my last book of poetry – I haven't decided yet. If it is, and if I can successfully kick the habit this time, then it will be a miracle. For every poet knows deep down, there is no escape.

And so, dear reader, I will leave you with the book. I hope you like it. I hope that you will allow it to breathe and that it will serve you in times of need, boredom and leisure. I also hope that you take in each of these pieces with a grain of salt and a heaping dose of reality and that maybe they'll make you laugh, think, pause or learn.

I wrote them not for you, but for me – this is, after all, my therapy and I have successfully excised yet another batch of malignant thoughts from my mind. I now present them to you, as a gift. Enjoy.

Thanks for reading.

- Santino J. Rivera
St. Augustine, Fla. September, 2017

ONE

fitting death for a pig

I like to imagine that Sheriff Joe
will one day choke to death
on a piece of half-chewed and greasy
Sonoran-style hot dog chunk
at some no-name shithole
in the middle of the desert
on a day hot enough to melt
hateful legislation
into puddles of sustenance
for those in need

It will all go down
in a place where
he harassed people he took for granted
on the regular
and they all know him by name
'Jefe Joe'
he'll waddle inside like some
Porky plantation owner
made of lard and maggots
and shit and paste
and grabass his way to the table
making sure the help knows
he's got them under his fat fucking thumb
winking and smacking his porcine lips
demanding service with a shit-eating grin
and "aw shucks" attitude

After they bring his plate out and
place it before his majesty's piggy little eyes
and he begins to shovel bite after bite
into his greasy food hole,
while reciting his own recipe for Nutraloaf
to a crowd waiting for him to croak,
he will clutch at his throat
with his eyes bugged out of their sockets
and he'll make those guttural choking sounds
you only hear in certain porno films

all while turning red as an Arizona ballot

Not a single soul there will lift a finger to help him
while he convulses and gags on the floor
writhing and jerking like the piece of shit that he is
dying before the ancient desert Gods
and a jury of his prisoner peers

A small boy will walk over to him
and toss a tepid glass of water on his face
causing no reaction
then be scolded for it
by elders who know
it is better
to let nature
take its course
and so, the sheriff will die like that
on the floor
in the middle of nowhere
wet and surrounded by those he hates
underneath a desert sun
in the middle of a land
which was Mexican once,
Indian always
and will be again,
with a giant piece of greasy
and half-chewed pork
wedged in his throat

A fitting death for a pig.

happy fifth of mayonnaise

Nobody knows how tough it is to be a Chicano
especially during the weird predicament
that occurs during the 5th of May(onnaise)
in the not-so-united-states-of-America
Chicanos, you see, are supposed to know
all the American holidaze
and also the Mexican ones too
but never the Chicano holidays
because we're not allowed to have those,
much less celebrate them
We can't even have our own books
(thanks Arizona & Texas and all the Falsos too!)
Beer? Si!
Libros? No!
It is confusing
so we all spend our time arguing with each other
over the significance of this or that
while the liquor companies rake in the cash
Mexico laughs
drunk frat boys play 'Pancho' with a big mustache
wasted frat girls play sexy, spicy Señoritas
and Rick Bayless makes something he calls "guac"
with fucking peas in it
24-hours go by and suddenly
no one wants to be Mexican anymore
not even your local news anchor
with the big clip on mustache and sombrero
at least until next year

Does Mexico celebrate the Chicano Moratorium?
Does America celebrate the Crusade for Justice?
No.
Mexico Mexicans do not even know who Cesar Chavez was
but neither do most red-blooded Americans
Does Mexico mourn Ruben Salazar?
Chale...
But Chicanos?
We're expected to know

and to mourn
and to let our gritos roar
ajua!
Lest we lose our street cred
or slink back into the pocho melting pot
of online bitterness
which never, ever ends
spending the rest of our days calling each other out
trying to out-Chicano one another
because as the prophet Abraham Quintanilla said
in a book of unspoken Chicana/o proverbs:

we gotta prove to the Mexicans how Mexican we are
we gotta prove to the Americans how American we are
we gotta prove to the Chicanos how Chicano we are

It's exhausting!

But at least we have the fifth of May

a place called hell

I was shown a photograph last night
of a man I know only through mutual relationships
It wasn't even a real photograph
but a picture on a phone
People can hardly be bothered with tangible things
these days
I wonder when that will apply to the soul,
or if it already does
Does Satan accept tweets?
but I digress

This man, whom I haven't seen for years
yet the last time I did,
he was singing Bob Marley
Redemption Song
His voice carried then and things were not
as they seemed
for the feelings in a man's heart
are never truly revealed
until the stakes are raised
He looks different now but certainly happy
And why not?
I was told that this man lives in a small town,
one you've never heard of,
between this side of Mexico
and that side of Damnation
They said that he charters private flights
for high-end clientele
Who, exactly?
No one knows
or says
The purpose?
He spots smugglers and the (not really considered) people you hear
all about
on the news so frequently
every time another asshole decides to run for President
These less human than humans you hear about
crossing through the Devil's Highway

on our very own version of the Hunger Games
for a shot at the proverbial brass ring

And this man, his clientele
Well, they do whatever it is they do
with that kind of information
you can probably figure the rest out for yourself
This is all private enterprise
hush-hush, not on the news
sold to the highest bidder type stuff
because where isn't there some kind of private enterprise
in this society
trying to make a buck from someone else's misery?
Ka-Ching!

The border patrol stays with swollen budgets and
feigned desperation
the private prisons turn soaring profits
the politics on both sides of the aisle are never
without self-serving fat to chew on
nor buttons to bush
and this guy,
this guy who's hand I shook once in my life
at some forced family function
with bitter smiles
well, he makes a very comfortable living
out there in the great AmeriKKKan wasteland
everyone pretends is merely fictional
yet real enough to vote on

So, what, right?
Well, the moral to the story is this:

don't give me any bullshit about
playing by the rules
or the rule of goddamn law
when it comes to that line in the fucking sand
which cuts through time and space
and beyond
from here to 1492 and backwards again

through history
For there are forces as work
Who not only burn crosses but
who serve those who would fill their hands
with gold
in exchange for the lives
of those seeking their next meal
or simply a drink of water

This is not a just country
It never can be so because it's on stolen land
and so we will watch it burn to the ground
one day
while the rich escape to the moon
and the meek shall inherit
a place called Hell

if 6 was 9

White collared Latino conservative
flashing down the street,
pointing their plastic finger at me
They're hoping soon my kind will drop and die,
But I'm gonna wave my Raza flag high,
High!

Sell on, sell on...sellout
Fall Hispanic businessmen,
just don't fall on me
Go ahead on Mr. Latino Marketer man,
you can't dress like me
Raza knows what I'm talking about

We've got our own lives to live
We're the ones that's gonna have to educate ourselves
when it's time for us walk the path to self determination
So let us read the books that we want to
Yeah...

Sing on Brother,
Play on Sister...

preface: /gwɑːtə'mɑːlə/

what do we know of /gwɑːtə'mɑːlə/
what does anyone
how much do they mention in the public schools, here
in college
on the street, in whispers
or maybe screams

That it was conquered by Spain
its people cast aside
while the land was raped
No.

That it became a so-called Banana Republic
a Los Norte Americanos
whom look down their noses
perched atop man-made borders
No.

That the C.I.A. helped to overthrow
the government and dismantle the country
effectively sending them back to the 1500s
once and again
forever
No.

That over 200 thousand people were killed
over a 30 year civil war
that the USA helped to wage
only to leave it as one of the most
violent countries in the world
with nothing more than an apology?
No.

They teach none of this
No one speaks of /gwɑːtə'mɑːlə/
except to say:

isn't that where all those gangs are from?

God, what a shithole...

And a hole in the world opens up
and sucks all the apathy down inside of itself
some might call it a rabbit hole
others a wishing well
but down we go and see how far
this disease from Amerikkka travels...

for Alma: hell is a place on earth/ por Alma: el infierno es un lugar de la tierra

[Hell is a place on earth
sometimes
and we all get what we deserve
in the end]

Alma: a woman's name
daughter, sister, mother...almost
a descendant of the Maya
her name means: the soul
though I am sure that she lacks exactly that much
if such a thing even exists
and I know she knows this because
Alma murdered people
in cold blood
she helped rape and
torture others
like herself
she did these vile things
all in the name of love!

Huh?
But...how can that be?
¿El amor?
How can "love" draw so much blood..?
because en los estados unidos
there is enough love to go around
and then some...

In Amerikkka, we export a twisted version of amor
wholesale!
to any third world hellhole that will buy it
like so many Happy Meals and armor piercing bullets
the love of yourself
the love of your barrio
the love of your block
your city, your state, your nation
Love!
Amerikkkan style

we love our guns and our gods
we love our football and fast food
our fast women and faster talking politicians
and we love ourselves to death
for it's our national pastime
this l-o-v-e
this culture of destruction that we gift
our neighbors with time and again
neighbors like Alma
like so many other women
in their own versions of Hell
seeking that which they wish to escape

blood in/blood out
love in/love out

survival of the fittest
the ones with the most heart
putting in work
punching the clock
vying for the love
of blood-stained streets
and homies in shallow graves
A history of violence
cradled Alma from birth to the death
of her soul
her stillborn child and beyond
because she chose to be like the men who abused her
rather than be victimized by them
Alma chose love
Amerikkka sends another love letter
out to sea, message in a jagged bottle
knowing that some small child somewhere
someone just like Alma
will find it on the sand
read it and take the instructions to heart...
right after she carves out the corazon of those
who would do her harm
but before anyone can point any fingers at Alma
or any of these daughters and sons of blood
you must first understand that

this is all a product of Amerikkkan ingenuity

all/of/it

it is our gross domestic product
and we excel at manufacturing it
packaging it
distributing it
marketing it
and consuming it
wholesale death
the tattoos, the slang, the apathy
the penchant for extreme violence
the self-loathing
and course, the love!
we birthed this
rather, this is a mass produced product
of what some would call
a comedy
others a tragedy
depending on political affiliations
both of which are gangs in their own respect
and both of whom claim
to love their constituents

During the late 90's
the Clinton administration deported
countless Guatemalan refugees
tens of thousands of desperate people who
fled from a country of death and
decades of war
where all they found was an instruction manual
on how to hate yourself and kill people
in 10 easy lessons
what do you think they brought back home with them?
from Amerikkka?
land of rape and honey
after we schooled them and then fucked them off
what were their souvenirs?
their trinkets?
all you need to do is listen to Alma's story to find out

because she will whisper dark love songs in your fat ears
while you close your eyes and she slits your neck again
people like to remember the Clinton administration for
blow jobs and saxophones
condom-covered cigar tubes and toothy smiles
the greatest economy and
all that white-washed Kenny G jazz
and so much LOVE!
but he should be remembered for other things
like NAFTA and fleecing of Amerikkka
the new genocide on the third world
and the invention of people like Alma,
precious Alma with her deep eyes
which you could drown inside of
from falling into a tunnel of death and love
Alma, who sheds tears for her victims yet
knows she carries her Hell with her
in every space she dwells
Alma, a victim since day one but also a patron saint
of killers and of women
who choose the sword
in the name of amor
Talking heads and demagogues will point to her with scorn
with their blood-dipped fingers
to these so-called slums with disgust
clucking their tongues saying:

See! We must keep this kind from entering
Amerikkka!
Abandon all hope ye immigrants who enter here!
We must prevent them from poisoning our soil
and spreading their seed!
We must exterminate them
and all those like them!
We must build a wall!
And then a wall on top of that wall
because we have to be sure!
Death to all who oppose us!

And their nationalism runs cold through the veins
of killers and murderers

Because these same people
these blood lusters and people hustlers
either do not know
nor do they care that it is

THEM

their own self-preservation
their own waste
their own cognitive dissonance
their own treachery
their own hatred
their own policies
their own cracked mirrors
that have created Alma
but no one wants to remember these things
they all just want to point fingers
or bury their heads in the sand and giggle
we can all watch the same film and hear Alma's story
we can listen as she describes her nightmares
we can empathize
maybe
or turn away in disgust
but what we can never do is forget
that for every action there is an equal and opposite reaction
we reap what we sow and we have sown so much
hatred and violence worldwide
that we could submerge the earth in blood by now
were it not for modern plumbing
All of our hate
all of our rage
all of our lies
all of our loathing
all of our treachery
all of our thievery
all of our neglect
all of our disbelief
all of our pride
it all goes down the drain
and we never think of it again
ever!

but it should be no surprise then that these same gutters
eventually come to an end
and empty themselves out into something else
and we have been ignoring our sewage for far too long

So do not pity Alma
Her's is but another wretched and warped story
from the red, white and blue
¡Amerikkka!
she has her scars and her burdens
and she will carry them to her grave
but you should pity yourself
and me
and everyone around you
who make excuses
or simply ignore the conditions
that create people like Alma
for she is us
and we are her
and there is so much goddamned blood
on all of our hands

and it never
washes
off

*for reference: http://lightbox.time.com/2012/10/29/alma-a-tale-of-guatemalas-violence/#end

me and marco down by the schoolyard

Let's compare myself and say,
little Marco Rubio
the scumbag senator from La Florida
who runs from his constituents
and was bested by a human Cheeto
Many people would say
that we are Latinos
But what does that mean, exactly?
Why you do you call yourself Latino?
What does that mean to you?
Do you even know..?

See, me and Marco:

We don't come from the same place
We don't eat the same food
not even close
We don't have the same customs
We don't celebrate the same ancestors
We don't even speak the same Spanish
We don't have the same politics
We don't worship the same God
His family emigrated here
mine has been here for centuries
So what is this magical
homogenous thing
that binds us together?
other than a Spanish surname that is
and or a shared past
with the same rapist colonizers?
We have absolutely NOTHING in common,
me and Marco,
down by the schoolyard
But tell that to the media

Tell that to the politicians
Tell that to the marketers
Tell that to the corporations

Tell that to the Census
Tell that to #Latism
Tell it to all of the wholesale rainbow
rah-rah whores
grabbing for dollars and making little sense
I am not Latino
I am not Hispanic
I am not Marco
I am Chicano

they'll let you stay if...

THEY say:

we'll let you
stay
if you fight our
wars
if you take our
vows
if you swallow yourself
whole
if you cut your
tongue
if your chill your
heart
it you give your
vote
if you sell your
soul
if you blue your
eyes
if you take up
arms
if you forget the
past
if your burn your
books
if you wrap yourself in the
flag
if you turn your
back
along the lines in the
sand
keeping others just like
you

Out

of codices and culture

The stone is cast
what we do now
is pick up
the pieces
of broken glass
and try not to bleed to death
from wounds
opened by extreme
prejudice
and the censorship
of an invisible people
who walk the lines
between a pejorative
and a falsehood
still lost in a world
of confusion, scorn
and manipulation
the paradox
endures!

You can fire a bullet
into my head
with weapons fashioned from
hate
you can lock me up
under charges of
dissent
ban my books, pictures and art
seal them away in boxes
to collect the dust of bigots
lie, cheat and steal
as your ancestors before you
but nothing you do or say
will erase these words
this history
these stories
this culture
La Raza!

Our modern codices
will not be burned
no history
is ever
illegal
We will endure!

no mystery

You believe whatever the fuck you wanna believe, ok?
Lord knows there's enough misinformation and
history re-writing out there to fill volumes
there's enough carpet baggers,
revisionists, fake news and con men
looking to make a quick buck on Raza's backs and spilled blood
Ruben Salazar was assassinated
There's no mystery
no curiosity
no unanswered questions
the cops murdered him
plain and simple
They wanted the man responsible
for giving a national voice
to the "troublesome" Chicana/o Movement
silenced
Guess what?
It worked
El Movimiento ain't been the same since

During that time the very word "Chicano"
was part of the national lexicon
Can you imagine that?
There were no "Latinx"
No Hispanics
and no self-loathing or identity crises
It was used by people like Spiro Agnew,
Hunter S. Thompson
and the Wall Street Fuckin' Journal
You can credit Ruben Salazar for a lot of that
Now?
Shit, the very word itself is taboo
Internet fodder and media toilet paper
as more and more people vie for
more politically correct terms
Chicanos from that era scared the fuck out of
The Establishment
Ruben paid the price for it

He's no martyr
but he was definitely the messenger
and They silenced him
like They did so many others during that era
Anyone who was perceived as a threat
to power was assassinated
or vanished
So fuck you!
and your "mysterious" bullshit
Fuck you!
and your lack of a "smoking gun"
Fuck you
period.
Ain't no mystery.

c/s

ain't no sunshine

The immigrant detainees
in Baker County, Florida
That is,
the illegal sub-human beings
locked up inside of concrete buildings
with no windows
no natural lights
no rights
no nada
these, less than people
who are guilty
of no more than crossing
an invisible line in the sand
built on centuries of rhetoric
lies, revisionism, banned history
hatred
and general assbackwardness
Yeah, well, most of these less than people
lack any kind of legal representation
whatsoever
you know, lawyers and or civil rights advocates
who would see them through the legal system
Instead, they are caged
like rats
away from view
24-hours a day
left to rot inside of their cells
for daring to seek out what is natural:
freedom

So, if you please
count the minutes the next time
you are whistling out in the open
with your children
some breezy Summer day
because for these less than people
who only make the news during election years
there ain't no sunshine

anytime, hey
The sun
the sky
the moon
These are things reserved
for convicted murderers and rapists
on various yards across this facade
of a for-profit prison nation

Dare to seek a better life
in the land of rape and honey
and they will lock you up
in Baker County, Florida
and other places too
they will erase your name
throw away the key
put you to work
for a fortune 500 company
making their products for free
and never let you out
so that you may drive up the stock value
for some rich asshole vacationing
in the Hamptons
who cares not about
people deprived sunlight
or their children locked in cages
but only the bottom line
because to him, and many others like him
they broke the law
and someone must always pay

picking sides

Trying to explain the trials and tribulations
of what it means to be Chicano
in the US of Fuckin A
to someone from another nation
is comical,
if not absurd
it's difficult enough trying to justify it
to other Amerikkkans or
MexiKans
Just pick a side!
Ha!
I would argue that we are at war
and have been for some time now
the bodies are there
the aggression
the oppression
the propaganda
and the wholesale lies
both sides push
back and forth
the death toll is high
death of the mind
death of the body
death of the soul
yet most of us pretend
as if it is not happening
because we, Chicanas/os!
are akin to the children
in an abusive household
watching our parents fight
with each other
pretending that we have loyalty
to neither one
or that anything is wrong
until they look away
the turmoil we feel inside is expressed
in our art, literature, song and dance
our confusion

our division
our daily desmadre
We are the children of a broken home
finding our own path
on a road
that don't exist
seeking self-determination and fighting
often times with ourselves
for a scrap of goddamn identity
which is often denied
stolen by some
sold by others
and some of us never find it
all the while the war rages on
at "home"

raza is raza

Someone told me Raza is a bad word now
for fuck's sake
Raza is Raza!
Look, I don't tell you what to call yourself
so don't tell me what to call myself
you bunch of crybabies
This whole homogenization movement
being pushed and pimped by
marketing savvy Latinos and Hispanics
and self-loathing Mexican Americans
is the same old bullshit
recycled from ages past
and handed down by those
who would undermine your own identity
for a profit

"It's not a race it's an ethnicity..."
Fuck outta here
I will tell you this:

I'm not White
Nor am I Black
Chinese
Filipino
Jewish
Japanese
Korean
Vietnamese
Native Hawaiian
Samoan
Or some kind of special snowflake
I embrace my indigenous roots
with open arms
but even still
I am not Native American

GASP!

I am Chicano
through and through,
which for me means
I am not like you!
Soy de Nepantla
Look it up on Google Maps, smart ass
it's right next to the hyphen
in between Mexican
and American
we don't fit into a check mark box, holmes
Raza is Raza
If you don't understand Raza
then leave Raza outta your mouth
I have not nor will I ever
mark "white" for my race
on any government form
nor will I ever
deny my own identity
just to be PC
and spare someone's feelings
I don't give a shit what the "hip"
politically correct thing is to do
Any group that has hating yourself
as a prerequisite
can go fuck itself
Fuck the Internet
and fuck you
I know who I am

Soy Chicano y que?

language of the ghetto

at home
they taught me english
so that I
could make my way
in the world of bigots
at school
they taught me grammar
so that I
would know the rules
of their language
in high school
they taught me to speak European Spanish
so that I
could be further separated
from my brothers and sisters
when I walked into the world as man
my tongue was no sharper than birth
I could not communicate
with my own people
any more than I
could relate to the people who taught me the rules

what being chicano is like online

these days online
whew!
lemme tell you something
it's a wall made of backs turned
with knives sticking out of the top and bottom
we are trampled by
marketers
politicos
revisionists
backstabbers
sellouts
all screaming their own Grito:

MMMMMmmmmeeeeeeeeeeeeeeeee!!!!!!!

Vengeance is mine!
so sayeth the lawyers
the salesmen
the social media gangs
the pan-Latinists
the social justice warriors
the hypocrites and bastards
the liars
the falsos and trolls
with tongues forked and barbed
in a virtual ocean of bloodshed
where anything but Mexican will do!
And people who do not
know their own name
will carve hashtags into
their own flesh and
forge codices
for "likes"
rather than declare their own existence
because it's not PC to assert your own existence

Cognitive dissonance
is a helluva drug, ese
fuck social media

what chicano studies is not

Ethnic Studies

does not equal Chicana/o Studies

Latino Studies

does not equal Chicana/o Studies

Latin American Studies

does not equal Chicana/o Studies

Hispanic Studies

does not equal Chicana/o Studies

Culturally Relevant Courses

do not equal Chicana/o Studies

Mexican-American Studies

do not equal Chicana/o Studies

People died for Chicana/o Studies to exist
We earned it
Why then do you think
so many people are threatened by the truth?

whenever I listen to little wing

whenever I listen to little wing
by Jimi
I am transported back to my own version
of Nepantla
my homeland
which is unlike yours
it is not like Aztlán
there are no Mexicanos there
no Tejanos either
no rancheras
no botas
no somberos
there are no Californios
no Burqueños
no forked tongues
no tattoos
no spoked wheels
no bullets
no Norte or Sur
no flags
no conquerors
no Raza cosmica
no latinx
no arguments
no sellouts
no falsos
no cholxs
no drama
a toda madre
o un desmadre
no cosmic Chicana/os
floating in the middle
of time and space
surrounded by violent splashes of paint
rivers of sacrifice
mountains of resistance
and oceans of poetry
with one massive fire burning

that both consumes and
rebirths everything
forever:
somos pocos
somos siempre
somos eternos

Nope.
It's just me there
in my room
with my guitar
and without any inkling
of an idea
of what I am supposed to be
and not be
as dictated
by everyone else
throughout history
who knows better than myself
about me
My music has always
given me more solace
and peace
than any movement
ever could

x's and @'s

Hey!
You!
Yes, you!
We're still trying to out Xican@ one another here in 2013
Oh, man!
There's nothing like getting told
you're not [X] because of [Z] criteria
This issue comes up time and again in the
so-called Xican@ community
and it's always the same old argument

But guess what..?
There's no Xican@ handbook!
I know, right?
There's no litmus test either
There's no secret handshake
no archaic list of requirements handed down
by the ancient Aztec council
and no experts or definitive authorities
shocking, I know
We all walk the path to self-determination
in our own way
or not at all
And we all come from different walks of life!
My onda might not be your onda
pos, orale
somos Raza
No one has the right to define you
Only you can do that
If you choose to identify as Chicano
then you already are on the path
There is no secret society
that sends you a membership card
or a plaque
or a secret decoder ring
Identifying as Chicano these days
is radical enough as it is
where everyone wants to tell you

who you are
don't believe the hype online, kids!

I am often reminded of stories
from people who were told at some point
in their lives
that they were not Chicana enough
and I swear
we are harder on each other than anyone else
on this goddamned earth!
Why?
None of these things make you
any less than another

My atheism does not make me any less of a Xicano
than you
My Spanish sucks
I don't do Danza
and I hate fuckin' Morrissey!
The horror!
Please, report me to the Xicano Police at once
porque
I've know Christian Chicanas
and Buddhist Xicanos
I've met queer Xican@s
trans Xican@s
and everything in between
I've known Jewish ones
spiritualist ones
and atheist ones too (rare!)

So let me share something with you
that should be fairly obvious:
Chicano is a state of mind
not a goddamn religion
or a cult
or a product you can buy
I have my own reasons
for identifying with the X
And they are my reasons alone

no one else's!
but I'll be damned if I let anyone else
tell me what I am
and what I am not

a poem about ameriKKKan foreign policy and mexico

Immigration from Mexico is
at net zero
think about that for a minute
after you mute the television
or put your phone down
this is well documented
but it's not like anyone reads
any more
some statistics even show
that it is in reverse
imagine that!
what these so-called
boots on the ground
and a 'great' wall
would really do
is ensure
that no one escapes!
We are already prisoners
of our own minds
we wouldn't want any
consumer bees walking away
from the honey pot
now would we?
No, of course not
Sit back
crack a frosty brew
while we scoop your brains out
and process them
into delicious
solylent green cheeseburgers
Sizzle...
and watch another reality TV program,
or is it a Presidential address?
they're indiscernible these days

A rose by any other name
would smell as sweet
as the scent of death

from a nation set in flames
cannibalizing itself
silently
while everyone looks away
How is it that McD's
offers breakfast all day
and every single media outlet picks it up
ad nauseam
but a bunch of Mexicans are buried
in mass graves in Tejas
and not a peep?
Were there ever thousands of
murdered women
buried in shallow graves
in the hills of Beverly
surely the world would know
but maybe not
Alas, we are NOT all "Mexican"
as people would lead you to believe
on Fakebook
and to casually assert as much
is but a joke
nobody is laughing at
but the dead

wetbacks and waterways

does it not strike anyone as
I dunno
odd
ironic
fucked up
typical
that a white woman can freely swim
from Cuba to Florida
and people cheer her on?
Never mind
that the wet foot dry foot
water beaner
immigration policy for Cubans
would have them dodging
the National Guard
and ICE
UNLESS they reached land!
and were promptly
wrapped in a flag
given a hotdog
and a bible
a ballot
and a cup of coffee
because Fidel pissed in some Cheerios
so long ago
during an era when a nation of
so-called (but not really) immigrants
executed their own Prez
in the name of [REDACTED]

Never mind that
ANYONE else
caught doing that
would be arrested
detained
caged
numbered
interned

buried
ignored
forgotten
Never mind that Cuba
is considered
an enemy of the State
nor that "we" have an illegal military base
and a gulag there
But yes, way to go
swimmer lady!
kudos and whatnot
Is a white man gonna cross
the Mexican border next
while people cheer him on..?
Will he hurdle the dead bodies
as he goes?
Breaking world records as he
leaps over rape victims
and those who died of heat exhaustion?
Bizarro World knows no bounds

After all
Hypocrisy is
AmeriKKKa's cup of coffee

guidos an injuns

I realize that it annoys people
who would rather read Gawker,
make snarky comments
and bury their head
in a pumpkin spice latte
with intricate foam artwork
but I find the new found resistance
to Columbus day rather refreshing
if not a little funny because
This was not always the case

It was not too long ago
in a land far, far away
that if you were not down with AIM
or the Chicano Movement
you would just passively accept
this so-called holiday
and never think twice about it
But now you have White men
discussing the
validity of the name "Redskins"
on Sunday Night Football
in between beer ads
This doesn't mean things are better now
but awareness is at least
a small step forward
or not

I remember the days
when the Italian community
would come out in force
in protest of the protesters
on Columbus Day
heads would roll
in the streets where
ideologies ran hard
Men of honor
doused our enemy's effigies in blood

and were met with the wrath
of white supremacy
You took a risk opposing those
who would celebrate the oppressors
and that made you feel alive!
because we didn't fuckin' do it
online only

But this
this is the digital age
and so the people express themselves
in keystrokes
which you could argue
is not really tangible
nevertheless,
I suppose it is still expression
But I hope that the kids today realize
that there is a world of difference
between pouring blood
on a statue of your enemy
and standing toe to toe
against those who would defend him,
than simply reblogging a meme
and citing it as gospel
for five seconds
of fame

I am not a taco

I am not a taco
I am not a bottle of Tapatio
I am not a bottle of Cholula
I am not a packet of hot sauce with a catchy phrase
I am not a Corona, a Tecate
or a bottle of tequila
I am not a daily especial con frijoles y arroz
or con goddamned sour cream
I am not illegal
I am not hispanic
I am not latino
I am not a voting bloc
I am not here
I am not there
I am not a statistic
I am not undocumented
I am not on the news
I am not at Home Depot
wearing tattered clothes
smeared in the dirt
waiting for the call of hard labor
I am not invisible
I am not in the fields
I am not putting food on your table
I am not cleaning hotel rooms
I am not cooking food at a trendy franchise restaurant
I am not a demographic
I am not a chess piece
I am not voting for you
I am not banned
I am not a big butt and a smile
I am not a firecracker
I am not hot-blooded
I am not in a gang
I am not in a cartel
I am the not a scapegoat
I am not a token
I am not a savage

I am not White
I am not uneducated

I am Xicano and I will endure.

it's not a victory

It's not a "V" for victory, vato
if Raza books are still banned

If Raza teachers are still fired,
then that is not a victory

If barrio schools are still closed
that is not a victory

If the very word Chicano is still taboo
that is not a victory

If the same school board
that did all of the above
now has the authority over Raza studies
and final say on what is allowed
and what is not
that is not a victory

Settle for nothing now
Settle for nothing later
Miss me
with your false flags and
shouts of: Victory!
and selfies
focused only on you
Call me
when the "revolution"
is no longer being Tweeted

There's this whole faction now
of Hispanics
pushing for assimilation into the vortex
of "mas"
mas marketing
mas media
and mas bullshit
They want you to Hispanicize yourself

They want you to shill for corporate products
They want your soul
and they want to pay you for it
Do not lose your identity
in this slave new world
Do not jump into
this sea of corporate and political pandering
Do not buy into
this endless marketing campaign
Do not turn your back upon the past
as they dig deeper holes
to bury it
Do not believe the hype
as so-called leaders sell us wholesale lies

And the wind whispers:
La lucha sigue

chicano poets

Chicano poets, rare and true
persist through decades of bullshit,
fear and self-loathing,
with their chins high,
if only to say:
¿y que?

chicano soul

It's that Chicano soul
when we love something
we love it to death
and when we hate something
we take it to the grave
It's a thin line

the chicano get down

I cannot get down
with most of my people
because I have broken too many rules
I have sinned too many times
and never forgiven those
who I have trespassed against
and who also have trespassed against me
I am repentless
Y que?

The first commandment I broke
was losing my tongue
at birth
then again countless times
over my life
as the rules changed
on which tongue I was supposed to use
The absence of my language
keeps me from having a voice
no amount of books or study
can give that back
and I remain mute
lost among my own
shunned for not sharing the same tongue

The second commandment I broke
was selling my soul for rock and roll
picking up the guitar
and not baptizing myself
in the waters of Chente, Morrissey
or oldies por vida
I was too metal for the raza
and too Chicano for the metalheads
Though I found salvation
At the church of Suicidal
My musical taste kept me
From worshipping at the house of mi gente

The third commandment I broke
was reading too many books
fucking schoolboy, they called me
you look like a professor, they said
mis lentes, I discovered opened my eyes
and closed others
I learned too many words
I spoke like a white boy
an academic
I found myself the only brown face
in a sea of white
and no matter how many words I learned
no matter how many books I read
neither my people nor the students
would accept me
porque there's nothing more awkward
than an educated Chicano
scorned by his own
ostracized by the institution
looking for an identity

The fourth commandment I broke
was losing my religion
The absence of God in my life
has kept me separated from friends,
from my family
and from my people
though I grew up Catholic
though I had my crucifix blessed
down at St. Dominic's on Federal Boulevard
I made the mistake of asking a priest one day
to explain to me the mystery of dinosaurs
his reply:
the lord put those bones in the earth
to test our faith
and ever since that day I have been an atheist
a heretic among my own, the faithful
who may profess to have love
for me
but also believe that one day I will burn

The fifth commandment I broke
was straying from the flock of political correctness
because I refused to drink from the same trough
as the two-headed monster
but all the cheering leading in the world
could not slake my thirst
for seeing through the bullshit
of a two-party monster
alas, I could no longer relate to my people
who would cheer for only one team
live or die
like gang colors
decade after decade
and see no grey area
or anything in-between
I cannot pretend to be something
I am not
nor support a system
who pretends that I don't exist

The sixth commandment I broke
was not marrying within my own race
you would think this
the deep south
100 years ago
causing a rift so profound
that my people might as well be
casting stones
for my sin
even though I was taught
not to judge a person based on the color
of their skin
but by their character
and the heart
inside
it pains me to see faces contort
sneers and jeers
even in jest
when this rule is violated, blatantly
because we have somehow wound the clock

back
The seventh commandment I broke
was that of my meals
sacred
my sustenance
my lifeblood
things handed down from generations
it turns out that the food I grew up with
is not as common as I thought
among the people
my food was blasphemy to many
and the more I traveled
the more I discovered that I ate my sins
for nourishment
my home recipes were a thing of scorn
and that nothing ever tastes like home

The eighth commandment I broke
was moving away from my people,
from my blood
from my friends and my enemies
my loves, my hates
the ones who shunned me
the ones whom I cursed
I moved so far away
to the edge of my sanity
to the middle of nowhere
where I never see anyone who looks like me
except when I travel
and when I do
I am reminded of all the rules I have broken
over the years
and of this cross I bear
which I am trying to burn
so as not to pass on this burden
to my children

The ninth commandment I broke
was not having any direct ties to the motherland
I'm not from Mexico

My parents aren't from Mexico
My grandparents aren't from Mexico
No one ever crossed the border
the border crossed us
so Mexico can kiss my ass!
And for this sin I am disowned
I have no tongue
no land
no history
no identity
for all of my life as a Chicano
I was taught to pledge allegiance to the motherland
a place I am not from
a place which holds no magic for me
I am from the hyphen
neither here nor there
a stranger in a strange land
And for my sin
I walk alone

The tenth commandment I broke
was growing old
The next generation has put me on the shelf
written me off
and left me for dead
an old man too stupid to understand
the nuances of the hip and woke
I am not woke
I am asleep
dusty
A dinosaur
from a different era
unable to relate to the young minds
who would slash and burn everything before them
which represents wisdom
repeating history
again
as the conquerors always erase
that which comes before
them

The last sin I will commit
will be death
And when I die
I will be called out
crucified
and put in my place
by the next generation
of sinners
saints
and all those in between
who are destined to
break the same rules
bury the past
and live free

c/s

TWO

end of the line

This is the ruca in my dreams
It's not what you think, ese
and I know what you're thinking, aye
Every time I jump in the '48
she gives me this pensive look
with those eyes
Mas firme
Chingona
Chauuu!
before pushing her stiletto on the gas pedal
as far as it will go
Each night we end up in a hail
of twisted metal
fire and blood spatter
¡quemando llanta!
on the highway at the edge of my mind
Each night I know better
and yet I always climb inside
and sit next to her
There are no words
between us
barely even a glance
the rush of the screaming wind
and trails of lights passing by
are enough to make my heart explode
Her name is on my lips
at the moment just before impact
and each morning I wake up
to echoes of her laughter

a poem for llewelyn

Beer leads to more beer
she said
in a thick west Texas accent
while pausing to look over her shoulder
with a wink
and a smile
before disappearing
deep
into the darkness
of another motel room
her lithe legs and ass
illuminated by the
neon sign
and the shadow of
death

goddess of death

She steps out of the ranfla
clouds of sweet smoke billowing
into open air
the song of the Goddess
fades away on the radio waves
her stiletto sparks the concrete below
in a flash
as the scene reflects
off of the chrome on her heels
the already spent bullet casings nearby
set the stage
street lights glint off of the barrel
of the revolver
expertly manicured fingers reveal
a touch of death
and trigger finger dreams
where a woman's work is never done
because a woman's touch is never won
through the cold blood
running away
like so much cheap mascara
on these streets
where mujeres pray
for their own salvation
and lay
heathen men
to an early grave

death is a mujer, part 4

Somewhere,
in some alternate universe,
I'm sitting inside the wreckage
of a 1965 Chevy Impala,
hardtop
waiting for the song to end
so that I can close my eyes
again
forever

And she,
L.A. mujer,
is stepping out,
unscathed and gorgeous,
dressed to kill
stiletto heels clack
on the asphalt
as she walks away from the wreckage
and strikes a single match
to light her smoke
Illuminating a wicked
black lipstick smile
chrome hoops
and just maybe,
a screaming skull,
in the flash of the cherry red
inhale,
exhale
boom.

the last love letter

I never knew exactly what to say to you,
mujer
I still don't
la Reina de la Muerte
Mictecacihuatl: Queen of Mictlan
I know that you could have killed me
all those years ago
with a flutter of your eyelash
a brush from your lips
whisper
a last caress
dead flower petals
falling from your hair
but at the moment of truth you hesitated,
Why?
I may as well be dead
for as long as it's been
since we shared some pisto
and each other's company
laughing inside of one another
pressing our souls together
"Beautiful but deadly..." they said
Would killing me softly have solved anything,
Ruca?
Except to sate the appetite of Nuestra Señora de la Muerte?
For she who loves with the heart of a Woman
also requires a heart sacrifice in return
sangre por sangre
blood in
blood out
I know you have thought about it
often enough with each sunset
reminisced about how you would have put my body
in the trunk of that ranfla
and left it at the bottom of the lake,
keeping my essence in a bottle
and swallowing the stars whole
by daybreak

I think about how maybe
I should have sent you one last love letter
Frank Booth style
to protect myself from your evil ways, bruja
But mostly I think about the wasted time
and my sacrificed heart
its blood running down the temple
of what we once called our love
I wish there was some way to get it all back
I'd kill you for it
if I really believed it was possible
But I know you're out there
somewhere, searching for bones
not quite a smile on your face
not quite a look of love either
Lady of the Dead,
in waiting
If we ever do cross paths again
just make it quick
porfas
and seal it
with a kiss

c/s

38 special and a bottle of olde e

The lights are low
and the music loud
the room is spinning 'round
laughter drifts in
from somewhere
and you crack
a smile for now
[instead of later]
everyone else is out back
watchale
38 special and a bottle of Olde E
Badass bitch sez:
where you think you're going aye?
I ain't even got started yet
and so time passes slow
with beads of sweat
as you wait for a kiss goodnight
maybe the right kind this time

THREE

no colored allowed

People of color
or "POC"
is modern code for 'colored'
which sits just fine with some folks
who don't mind the chains
of their self-imposed oppression
because they don't think of it
in terms of segregation
or separate but equal
but it is
no different
than the "colored" signs
from a different era
which seems to be making a comeback
only this time
it's the opposite
History does indeed repeat itself
all those bigots in the black and white photos
from decades ago
would be amused to see they have
friends of the opposite color
here in the so-called
information age
where we're just a few steps away
from "POC only" water fountains
next to the gender fluid toilets
housed inside of the Non-Trump Voter grocery stores
inside of the FEMA camps
Becky is code for white bitch
Thug is code for nigger
Latinx is code for cult
Hispanic is code for sellout
Yt is code for honkey
Wypipo is code for crackers
Straight white male is code for piece of shit
PC is code for fascism
Feminism is code for misandry
SJW is code for Nazi

Nazi is code for everything you disagree with
CisHet is code for self-loathing
Commie is code for faggot
Liberal is code for Reagan-era republican
GOP is code for Reagan-era extremists
Fascist is code for a word losing all meaning
Green frogs are code for literally Hitler
Russia is code for humping the leg of McCarthy
OK is code for white pride
what's your code?

an outrage

When you're young and Brown
in the not-so-united states of America
you learn early on
what the police
are all about
maybe not immediately, mind you
but eventually
it is sometimes taught
with blunt force

As parents, we teach our children
different lessons
about the thin blue line
that exists to separate Them
from Us
The indoctrination starts early
even before formal schooling
or first steps

Trust them
They are your friends
They will help you
Etc.

And all of that is torn down
just as quickly as it was established
in a flash of blue and red
or a blinding white light in your eyes
on the side of the road
some random night
where no one
can hear you scream,
except maybe a camera
which may or may not be "lost"
and will most definitely be debated
online
by armchair lawyers
and civil rights wannabes

standing in traffic

It's bizarre watching this kind of thing
unfold, or rather
spill
unto the minds of those so young
this thing called uniform worship
which we teach, preach
and reach for
whenever something bad happens
in relation to a person
donning a badge
and some person whose life
may or may not matter

It is surreal watching children memorize things
like the Pledge
filled with words they cannot comprehend
yet know by heart
It all goes over your head as a kid
I sang the Pledge
I folded the flag
I thought cops were the good guys
and then it happens one day

You get stopped
frisked
blamed
bounced
questioned
called names
your picture is taken
your name gets put on a file
you get roughed up
humiliated
killed
sometimes for nothing
and it's only the beginning
the humiliation lives on forever
on the web

Many of us have countless stories
of why the cops are about anything but
help
These stories get passed on
from generation to generation
and then those kids start chalking up
stories of their own
My generation watched Rodney King
get beaten half to death
on TV
Then we watched the world burn down
after the cops who did it
were acquitted
Nothing has changed
except that maybe even more people
are brainwashed now
into thinking a uniform makes you
a good
or bad person

My children play in the background
while the news of Christopher Dorner
blazes across the screen
and the trigger-happy cops
who poured the gasoline
on the log cabin he was in
are never questioned about shooting
hundreds of bullets
into a truck
putting holes into civilians
caught in the crossfire
at the corner of Bad Luck Ave.
and Amerikkka St.
while the boys and girls in blue
hunt for one of their own

So then you teach your children
an extra lesson
about the police:

Watch out
Be careful
Don't make any sudden moves
Be polite
Use your camera
Know your rights
They are not your friends
Don't trust them
Don't be fooled by the uniform
They are just people
like any other
and all people have flaws

You wait and hope that something
doesn't happen to them
ever
because I still get nervous
every single time
I see cops
in the rear view mirror,
which is ridiculous,
all things considered,
but then again, maybe it's not
I mean, just look at the headlines

The abuse is so prevalent now
it's passé
I wonder where the legislation that protects
Us from Them
is?
but then I remember
that hope and change
are for fools
same as shitting in one hand
and wishing in the other

Perception is a bitch
Here in the so-called
Information Age
where people pick and choose their reality

like their produce
no fake apples, please
the police
and how they are perceived
is one of those great hidden Amerikkkan truths
that only part the population has any idea about
the rest never learn what it's like
to fear the police
instead of run to them for help
They will never know
the knot you get in your gut
when you are wondering
just how far
officer friendly wants to push the envelope
or what it's like
to get your ass kicked
and hauled to jail
for not signing the back of a parking ticket
that you paid the fine for

But then I remember who makes the laws
And that it's only
justice for some
I also remember that
It is impossible to define the word
"justice"
If ever, these legislators
or their children,
high in their ivory towers,
find themselves on the receiving end
of a nightstick
some crisp evening
when they have nothing on their minds
but the trivial pursuit
of happiness
on this giant plantation,
I shall not want
for revenge
but instead
perspective

acknowledgement
that maybe we should not fear our public servants
but that our public servants
should fear us

That,
after all,
would be an outrage.

a poem about gated communities & the children who walk through them

I watch a child
march down the street
he is silent but not cautious
donning full camo gear
and a black, plastic machine gun
with an orange tip
(for safety)
that he occasionally points at
passersby or cars, and houses
Rat-a-tat-tat!
Pop! Pop!
Bang! You're dead!
And all I can think of is:
goddamn they start wanting war earlier
every year

And then
as the sun passes behind the clouds
on this Sunday morning
where I have not yet
read of the latest child
to be murdered in the streets
I think of other kids
walking through a similar neighborhoods
armed with only small pieces of candy
sugary drinks
and maybe the color of their skin
which is a weapon now,
though not by choice
and all I can think of is:
goddamn they kill them younger
every year

And I close my window shade
as if it has the power
to block out the world,
slump back down into my comfortable chair

where I can only hear
the sounds of children
playing war
until the night comes again
bringing with it
more death

a poem about gun rights in amerikkka

Once upon a time
a group of lawful Black men
took their machine guns and pistols
and strapped them
to their bodies in a grand display of
freedom

They went to their local Starbucks
to exercise their constitutional right to bear arms
and enjoy some coffee
The police, FBI, DEA, NSA and The National Guard
were called immediately
by several patrons, onlookers
and every single employee,
mother and child
within a 20-mile radius
More than a few people fainted
and one white woman screamed:
"Won't someone please think of the children!?"

The pigs, acting upon instinct
and centuries of hatred, racism
and good ole AmeriKKKan know how
surrounded the coffee shop and
secured all of the white people before
firing several hundred thousand rounds into the place
and then lit the building on fire,
while a few police tanks shot mortar rounds inside
making sure that all of the Black men died

Everyone outside danced
there were fireworks and a subsequent barbecue
with music, balloon animals, pony rides and cotton candy
All of this was caught on film
It went viral
There was a documentary about it
and there were several Fake NEWS pundits
who talked about

how the pigs needed counseling
for the stress they endured that day
for their bravery
and sacrifice to this great nation

Not a single pig was charged
with a crime
no laws were changed
several flowery speeches were made
and tears shed on national TV
There were several hashtags created
to express on-line outrage
over the injustice
but no one could agree exactly
which injustice
The news eventually died down
and everyone moved on
But there's a museum now
and a gift shop
to commemorate the bravery
of the armed forces that day
who dealt with the enemy
of the state
you can buy a commemorative cheese platter
that says,
"Never Forget"
on it
with the images of the cops erecting a flag
on the burnt corpses
of the Black men who dared
to exercise their rights that day
at Starbucks

The End.

hashtag blow me

Nothing changes
people change places
and switch roles
but the song remains the same
We endure the same injustices
decade after decade
and just call it something different

No, scratch that
We endure it
but these days
we Tweet about it
Snap it
put it on the Gram
and then chalk that up to
"progress"
somehow

That's considered activism
now
which is pretty fuckin funny
considering how
real blood-soaked history
is not so distant
but here,
sign an on-line petition
Here, signal boost this
Here, read this thread
Here, tag this
Here, selfies for justice
Here, get your Meme PhD
Here, follow me
Here, blow me

It all amounts to self-gratification
mental masturbation
which is nothing new
but goddamn there is a lot of cum

¡gentrify this!

What's so bad
about gentrification anyway
you know?
when cities refuse
to put any kind of resources
into fucked up neighborhoods
until the property values rise
and the White folks move in
then all of a sudden
there's a community center
and the city is suddenly
cleaning the park again!
there's a playground
and basketball nets
in the hoops
are all present
instead of caddy corner
so as to discourage a pick-up game
from men
a darker shade of blue
Who knew!
Garbage collection
and officer friendly too
walking the beat
Wowsers!
What's that?
No more corner liquor store?
No more gun shop
No more "adult" store
just outside the school zone?
My, my…must be the nice
white folks moving in
Gawd bless 'em and
watch them home values rise
until you can no longer afford
the property taxes
I would love to see
gang injunctions

in White neighborhoods
that have meth houses,
skinheads and bikers
KKK uniforms in the closets
and White picket fences
I'd love to see cops
shake down the local soccer moms
and gossiping blue hairs
walking their Peruvians
and allowing them to shit on the lawn
The pigs would go through their purses
and diaper bags
looking for drugs and weapons
of mass destruction
Let's shake down that old man
mowing the lawn!
He looks like a terrorist!
Yeah, that'll never happen
So you might as well enjoy the trade off
of a neighborhood
on the rise
until the day comes where
you no longer recognize it
and find yourself on the outside
looking in
when you can't go home no more
Gentrify this, mother fucker

come to heaven (it's whiter here!)

Come to heaven
It's Whiter here
(Psst...nicer here)
No Blacks
No terrorists
No Indians
No Chinese
No illegals asking: por favor (that means 'please')
Steve Jobs is here!
The Macho Man, Ryan Dunn
Elvis and John Lennon too
Ronald Fucking Reagan, Liz Taylor
John Wayne and Charlton Heston
All have paid their dues
Pearly gates, pasty cherubs and wait...
(Um, no...those people are down there. Yes, there...)
Anyway, rejoice!
Hallelujah! We have Wi-Fi
And Starbucks
And pie!
And of course, the latest iPhone
And all the privilege you can shake a cloud at
It's really, really, really nice
We all sit-in and laugh and dance
and craft and play forever and a day
we are the people who keep heaven bright
We, the 99%
who are always White (and right!)
so when it's your turn to enter the gates
make sure your skin is just the right shade
for we all know that those who's pigment is less than perfect
are never seen (and never heard from)
White is divine
White is sacred
White is eternal
White is sated
Amen.

the st. augustine movement, 1964: a poem

I live here
I've fished here, surfed, broke bread
started a family
here
where there are ghosts everywhere
and not just of civil rights warriors
but of conquistadors and slaves
heartbroken Natives and gleeful mass murderers
domestic terrorists in white sheets
all trying to tell you their history
because civic leaders have tried to
hide it
bury it
drown it
erase it
change it
put in on the so-called bad side of town
while hawking trinkets
maps and train rides
creating a tourist industry around a place
that conquered
divided
and saw not so human people
sell human beings like cattle
and so we continue on in this so-called paradise
blind, deaf, dumb
watching not so historical reenactments
soaking up the rich HIStory
while tossing wishful coins into fountains
and dining where bloodshed and tears have stained the earth
waiting for the hand of God
to wash it all away

there's no such thing as reverse racism!

There's no such thing as reverse racism!
said the White slave to the Black plantation owner
Yeah, that's true, boy
the Black plantation owner said
Now get your White ass back work!
Crack goes the Master's whip
and away we go

There's no such thing as reverse racism!
said the White indigenous tribal leader to the Red colonizers
We know!
they said in turn and smiled
and burned several of the White people in a fire
Crack goes the wood burning in the fire
and away we go

There's no such thing as reverse racism!
said the White kid who was face down on the concrete
with the knee of a Black police officer in his back
I know that, bitch
the Black cop said
as he shot the White kid in the back
Crack goes the round from the barrel of a gun
and away we go

There's no such thing as reverse racism!
shouted the White indigenous farming community in Iraq
We know!
said the Middle Eastern pilots who were dropping
several tons of explosives on the White man's land
Boom goes the ignition of a warhead
and away we go

There's no such thing as reverse racism!
said the deformed White fetus in a jar to the Vietnamese scientist
I know that already,
he said and turned to burn more evidence of chemical warfare
Boom goes the volatile chemicals in the blaze
and away we go

There's no such thing as reverse racism!
screamed the White Zoot Suiter to the Mexican Navy Men
We know that!
they said and chuckled
as they beat him, stripped him and raped his wife
Crack goes the sound of a cranial fracture
and away we go

There's no such thing as reverse racism!
said the White Natives as they gasped for breath on dying land
we know said the Red military men
as they bulldozed a row of government housing
to make room for a mega-mall
Smash goes the sound of cheap housing collapsing
and away we go

There's no such thing as reverse racism!
said the elderly White man carrying his groceries
we know, honkey, said the jack-booted kids
from the Black skinhead gang
as they kicked the shit out of him and spray painted
'Whitey Go Home' on his garage
Psssssst goes the paint from the spray can
and away we go

There's no such thing as reverse racism!
said the elderly woman boarding the bus
the White driver looked at her and said:
I know, Cracker get in the back of the bus!
The wheels of the bus go round and round
and away we go

There's no such thing as reverse racism!
said the little White girls burning to death
in their church
We know that!
said the Black men throwing the Molotov cocktails
Wail goes the cries from the White church
And away we go

There's no such thing as reverse racism!

whispered the White man hanging from a tree
I know, said the all Black jury that convicted him
Of a crime he did not commit
as tied the noose round his neck
Shhhhh whispers the strange fruit
and away we go

There's no such thing as reverse racism!
cried the White man on death row
who was refused clemency
We all know that already
said the Black warden
As he pulled the switch
Bzzzzzzzt goes the sound of justice system
and away we go

There's no such thing as reverse racism!
yelled the crowd of White people
detained for not having their papers
we know that already, shut up!
replied the Mexican guards readying the trains to take them away
Toot-toot goes the sound of the train whistle
and away we go

There's no such thing as reverse racism!
cried the disproportional number of White men in jail, in unison
We know that!
replied the chorus of Black and Mexican judges
Boom goes the sound of the gavel in court
and away we go

There's no such thing as reverse racism!
moaned the students in the European history class
we know that already!
said the Arizona school board
as they boxed up their history books and banned them
the sound of censorship was so loud
the silence was deafening
and away we go...

never forget

Never forget
or so they say
so the bumper sticker reads
the t-shirt
the tattoo
the timeless classic on network tv
the banners
the ribbons
the parades
the monuments
the pages of the history books
never forget
the day the towers fell and buried
the rest of history underneath it
never forget wounded knee
never forget the emancipation proclamation
never forget 3/5ths of a man
never forget the treaty of guadalupe hildalgo
never forget slave plantations and bondage
never forget small pox infected blankets
never forget sour deals, free lunch meals
or public school no. 23
never forget joaquin murrietta's head in a jar
native skin with battle scars
the assassination of Che
of MLK
of Malcolm X and all the rest
never forget manifest destiny
never forget Timothy McVeigh
never forget all the bodies buried
in the Aztlan desert
never forget lines drawn in the sand
stolen land
shackled hands
never forget 1492
the demonetization of so-called savages
and invented gods and rules
never forget bombs over Bahgdad

over Japan, Iran, Afghanistan and abroad
never forget the secret wars
the crack cocaine
nor the profits reaped from them
never forget the lynching
the wholesale murder of the People
never forget the people of the sun
sb1070 and the detention camps
never forget operation northwoods
never forget operation wetback
the patriot act
nor the lies perpetuated to pass it into law
never forget the occupation
the indoctrination
the riots, the tear gas and wool being pulled over the nation
never forget
never forget
never
forget
ever
because the first casualty in any conflict
is always the truth
remember that

the ballad of troy davis

Death looms in Georgia
like a ghost from another era
welcoming parishioners, protesters and producers
to taste yet again
the strange fruit
live on the set of death row
and sponsored by doubt, rage and indifference
it all goes down on a Wednesday evening of censored truths
and ill consequences
where we learn time and again
there is no justice
just us
If all the world's a stage
then all eyes on the Peach state
on this date: 09:21:2011
where a man waits to bate his last breath
face his accusers and say:
I am Troy Davis and I am a man
despite what you say
there is more than a reasonable doubt
I am not guilty of this crime
blood be on your hands this night
and may God have mercy on your soul
and teach the world that
not all the king's lawyers
nor all the king's men
not even millions of supporters
could put Troy Davis back together again
because it takes a nation of millions to prove
though the days of tree hangings may be in the rearview mirror
when they want you dead
you will die 1,000 times
and again until
the crowd is pregnant with doubt
Full dark, no soul
full dark, no soul
full dark
no soul

the 13th amendment

"The Thirteenth Amendment to the United States Constitution abolished slavery and involuntary servitude, except as punishment for a crime."

except as punishment for a crime
except as punishment for a crime
except as punishment for a crime
except as punishment for a crime
except as punishment for a crime
except as punishment for a crime
except as punishment for a crime
except as punishment for a crime
except as punishment for a crime
except as punishment for a crime
except as punishment for a crime
except as punishment for a crime
except as punishment for a crime
except as punishment for a crime
except as punishment for a crime
except as punishment for a crime
except as punishment for a crime

stand your ground

Was there anything more polarizing than
standing your ground?
Yes, actually
Who knew that polarizing issues were
only getting started?!
This case
for its time in the spotlight
became the new Mason-Dixon Line
but it was only the beginning
and that line now changes on a daily basis
which seems implausible
but here we are
fighting this invisible civil war

You cannot define "justice"
any more than you can define
love or hate
which dictates that terms like
"social justice"
and "hate trumps love"
have lost all meaning
if they ever had any
because the war of words wages on
and we all pretend
that things that are subjective
are anything but
and anything objective
is up for debate

These days "justice" resembles revenge
because do unto others
as they have done unto you
has replaced the golden rule
in schoolhouses
from sea to shining sea
and we find ourselves
hurdling backwards through time
one act of "resistance" at a time

where nearly everyone is blind
because an eye for an eye
sells more news than
think for yourself

Young people
standing in the middle of a busy highway
during rush hour
eager to drive their point home
by blocking the path of working class folks
on their way home
find themselves at odds with those
who would otherwise agree
because who wants to be
on the "wrong" side of history,
right?
Even if it means
cutting your nose off to
spite your own face

Maybe
justice should mean
people throwing their television sets
out the window
and lighting their phones
on fire
or people throwing down
their weapons
leaving their barbed tongues behind
and finding things like compassion,
empathy and understanding
instead of fear and loathing
Maybe it looks like
people amassing to vote
without shame and
purging the legislature
watering the tree of liberty
and putting people into office
who actually give half a shit
about their constituents

Maybe,
in a perfect world
the Zimmermans of the world
wouldn't have so many fans
Women like Marissa Alexander
would be free
and Oscar Grant
along with countless others
might be alive
But we do not live in
a perfect world
We live in Bizzaro World
Justice?
There is no justice
just us
just you
just
I
And people forget
their own history
sometimes on purpose
sometimes for profit
but especially when history is buried
and destroyed
by corporations and politicians
and folks online
looking for a quick buck
and their 15 minutes
of InstaFame

People often say,
"Why do you always interject race?
That was a long time ago!"
But really, the past is never that far away
these kind of wounds never heal
especially when instead of learning from them
we just reverse the roles
and enact justice
in order to achieve satisfcation
You say plantation

I say private prison
You say officer of the law
I say overseer of the fields
You say lynching
I say the AmeriKKKan judicial system
You say move on
I say never forget
You say "nigga"
He says nigger
I say context matters
But maybe we should all take a cue
from Morgan Freeman
who is just an actor with a point of view
and shut the fuck up
about all of this stuff
for once
A moment of silence
could be turned into a
movement
Or maybe not
Who knows?
For the time being we are all content
to tear each other to pieces
in the name of
our new god
whom we hold
in the palms of our hands
waiting to tell us
what to think

FOUR

you can't hear bob seger

If White people cannot hear Jimi Hendrix
then Black people cannot hear Bob Seger
It's only fair

Bob Seger is for when you're at the roadside dive bar, 20 miles from
anywhere civilized, staring down the barrel of 10 years of sobriety
and riding wave after wave of intoxication right on down the god-
damn sewer.

Yee-haw, mother fucker and another.

Bob is for when you left everything you knew on fuckin' fire and
then walked off into the sunset to douse yourself in unholy water
and then strike a match.

Fwoosh!

Goodbye marriage.
Goodbye children.
Goodbye suburban wasteland.
Goodbye, Moon, you motherfucker!

Wake to the Devil's boot in your mouth and maybe a busted eye
socket; neon dreams and succubus screams, the world twists itself
right round and back upside down.

Cotton mouth ain't got nothin' on jumping off the wagon with both
barrels cocked and loaded. Boom, motherfucker!

And so you fall from grace and roll down the hill like so much shit
before you. You end up in a cold and dank cell waiting for your
fuckin' phone call. Just like every other asshole that thought he
knew the difference between a mortgage and a contract for your
soul.

That's what Bob Seger is for.

the worst television show of all-time

On the season finale of
The worst television show of all time!

tell them what they've won, Bob!
it's a neeeeeewwww war!!!!!!!!

[the audience explodes]

I feel like the government
congress
this administration
the President
the three branches of
Go Fuck Yourself
whatever the fuck you wanna call it
is like a reality television show that
has been on the air for far too long
maybe produced by Aaron Spelling
or something similarly wretched
hosted by Ryan Seacrest
filmed on location
on an Indian burial ground
and sponsored by a lite beverage
this terrible show that we are all
addicted to watching
and talking about
until it kills us
it needs to end
I don't wanna watch the next season!
Fuck this program!
Time to turn the TV OFF
I've talked about shooting my TV before
and being prosecuted for treason
for doing so
hard labor and probation
with a court order to buy another TV
just as soon as I'm "free"
so as to allow this programming to continue

but it's only gotten worse
and now
we have elected another TEEVEE star
to lead this shipwreck to its
final season, aptly titled:
FUCK YOU.

this is what we do now

This is what we do now
We bathe in blood
feign outrage
make idle threats
we "mourn"
we forget
we fuck
ourselves
as the media vultures
feed their young
the bleeding hearts and warped minds
of the selfie generation
tragedy after
so-called tragedy
24-fuckin-hours-a-day-we-never-close
the ignorance vomits itself
again
and again
and again
until we're spoon-fed
on a daily basis
like a bird feeds its young
regurgitating the "news"
into our hungry little minds
what is worthy
what is "news"
what is "fake"
and what deserves the holiest of holy
our thoughts and prayers
{ANGELS SING}
that you flush into the internet toilet
every single fucking time
some atrocity floats across your screen
These things
blood
and money
and death
and cum

and shit stains
and lies
and hashtags
and paid advertisements
and a Russian hiding in your closet
these things make the world go 'round
Get some!

howl (with apologies to a. ginsberg)

I saw the best minds of my generation
destroyed by marketers
cognitive dissonance
confirmation bias
starving hysterical naked online
dragging themselves though the digital streets at dawn
looking for an angry fix
to push in their veins
box frame tattooed hipsters burning
for the ancient cultural appropriation
starry-eyed starlets caught in the carnivorous
gears of the Hollywood machine
devouring culture whole
spitting it out
at a premium!
hollow-eyed audiences in the night
with false ideas of what it means
to be Brown in AmeriKKKa
in the supernatural darkness
of blue-lamp television sets
glowing across the tops of cities
contemplating suicide
for those who bared their souls
to Heaven under watchful eyes and ears and saw
prostitute angels falling and burning
on tenement roofs illuminated
because all who pass through Heaven's Gate
must be white as snow
and twice as rich with radiant blue eyes
hallucinating a rerun of Leave it to Beaver
where the only tragedy among the scholars of war
is how many times
Ward has slept with June
in the same bed

kill yourselfie

prologue: the internet sucks.

1

The world ends not with a bang
but 140 characters at a time
We have mutated into Eloi
we are technically adept
but we don't understand the technology
we have regressed
unlearned a millennia of culture
thought and reason
in exchange for convenience
and shackles
we are satisfied with the pleasure of merely existing
The 1-Percent are the Morlocks
and they eat us alive every single day
no one minds much though
cuz they teach us not to mind
so as to pique our curiosity
for whetting their appetite

I don't give a shit what you wore this week
I don't care what you ate
I don't give a fuck about your new shoes
Fuck your weight loss
Fuck you and your outfit of the week
Shove your hashtag up your ass
I'm sick of Instagram models
and Twitter philosophers

"everything I learned about the revolution I learned in 140 characters or less!"

How many selfies does it take
to get to the center of a Shitsie Pop?
You ever notice how we rally together
behind the wrong things all the time?

Real injustices go unchecked forever
but if there's a politically incorrect
TV show
Or celeb who says "nigger"
A racist Commercial
Nazi potato chips
Twitter accounts that are literally Hitler!!
Watch out!
We're easily pacified, dumb animals
sucking at the sweet, sweet nectar
of idiocy
inside of our hamster cages
Sit down
Shut the fuck up
And watch these messages
This mess for the ages
Sit down
Eyes and ears
Here
Attention
Actung!
After these messages
We'll be right back!
Here
Watch
Buy this

2

Skynet take me away
I could live without the Internet
or whatever you want to call it
I'm not sure what it is anymore except a distraction
a thief
a warehouse of lost minutes
hours and days
a pusher of false ideals
post truths
a spinner of realities
a wonder of technology gone horribly wrong

in a world where the future is now
and the age old question of:
What would it be like to know what everyone is thinking?
Well...now we know
and it's fucking horrible!
we have created a prison of our own making
in such a short amount of time
as we if have never done anything differently
or thought outside of this
[imaginary box]
Lo, the internet and social media came to us
starving artists
like some savior upon a cross
Woe, how It has left us
strung out and wasted
in search of the next fix and false idols

I have lived without such convenience before
I could live without
Google
Facebook
Tumblr
Twitter
I would survive without
RSS feeds
instant messages
YouTube
I could face each day without
blogging
or a godforsaken "smart" phone
I do not need to know what strangers
are thinking to enrich my life
each waking minute of the day
Such a concept is absurd
I could visit the local library again
or browse a bookstore
purchase goods and services locally
support small businesses
read a newspaper and write an angry letter
listen to the radio

or talk to real, living-breathing people
such a concept seems radical in this crazy
upside down bizarro world
we live in

You, yes you! could call me on the phone
write me a letter
knock on my door
or simply leave me be and we would all be OK
without each other
without this invisible connection so many deem necessary
we could all unplug ourselves at once
walk outside and say: Hello!

None of us really needs "the Internet"
or whatever it disguises itself as these days
a companion, a parrot, an instigator, an ally, a lover
but I suspect all of this worrying is for naught
and we will continue on in this myopic version of reality
where misery loves company
fooling ourselves into believing that any of this
has meaning

3

An imaginary philosopher once said:
most people are not ready to be unplugged
many of them are so dependent upon the system
they will fight to protect it
If you're wondering what's wrong with the world
just look at your phone

What's more addictive?
cigarettes or social media?
heroin or hashtags?
meth or memes?
I don't know how to Social Media
I never did
The entire time I was faking it
I'm a fruad

A faker
A sham
An imposter
A charlatan
A quack
A con man
A phony
A fuckup
A leftover from another era
A throwback

Everything ended up just like it did in high school
with all the different groups
talking behind all the other's backs
the popular kids
teacher's pets
the jocks
the misfits and social outcasts
all vying for the self-gratification
and the adoration of our peers
as we once did
so many moons ago
It's ridiculous how we
repeat the same social situations over
and over again
at different stages of life
until we're all dead
this life was not meant to be
experienced vicariously
yet here we all are
peeking into each other's windows
like a buncha fuckin' perverts
The future...I tell ya
who knew?

I have created so many windows by now
I lost count
Burned as many bridges with people
I never met in real life
yet in fake, online life this is

somehow more dramatic
Everyone projects who they are
all the cards are on the table at all times
all bets are off
stakes are high
call your bluff
what's the worst that can happen?
Nothing
None of it is real
I've burned more bridges than I can count
and had more burned before I ever came to pass
by people I don't know
this is nuts
what the fuck are we all doing
living inside of our heads?

I'm bad at this stuff
I can admit that
I don't have a Facebook
or a Snapchat
a Tumblr
or a next best thing
I've soured friendships with real people
over trivial discussions about nothing
and ended up laughing at how seriously
some of us take this goddamn thing
I don't know my gender pronouns
I have no clue if I'm a heteronormative
cis gendred white privileged Bernie bro
with transphobic, anti-black, misogynistic, homophobic
sparkle dust in my eyes
because no matter how hard you try
you cannot please all the snowflakes
all of the time
we have painted ourselves into a corner
where nothing is very much fun anymore!
as old Pink would say
Are you a fat-shamer?
A hypno-toader?
A 4-chaner?

Do you even tumblr bro?
I am a giver-upper
I want out
I want to exit through the gift shop and run
I want no part of it
I want to find a physical manifestation
of Social Media and
burn it to the fucking ground

4

It's absolutely fucking creepy
how many children have been brainwashed
to lick the boots of the state
via social media indoctrination
I mean
if you woulda told me 20 years ago
that in the future
children would be telling adults
that graffiti is "wrong" because it's "bad"
or that college kids would be
stomping people in order to
subvert the freedom of speech
I'da told you to fuck right off
Hell, I'm here right now
telling these children to fuck off!
What a weird, fucked up, upside down
world we live in right now
And I think part of maturing in this death throe
here in the year of our lord Cthulhu, 1492
is letting go of "news" sites like
Gawker
Vice
Cracked
Huffington Post and so on
Facebook
Buzzfeed!
Various bloggers and social media celebrities
I need absolutely none of it
We have turned the internet into

the waste bin behind McDonald's
I no longer peruse any of these things
I simply let them go
and I let more and more go each passing day
And this is not to say that there are
better alternatives, because really
everything sucks right now
But the longer I stay plugged into the ol' Matrix here
the less I hold on to
in the tangible world
They
the proverbial They
can have it.
It's all so unnecessary and pointless
And dead
It feels like a graveyard online

Protesters policing other protesters
blogging about protesting social media
protesting on tumblr via facebook
and trending on twitter
but then on IG
and then on Vine for a demonstration
against the police
on the next Maury
Plot twist: Some of the protesters are cops
some of the cops are protesters
Double plot twist:
you ARE the father!
People telling other people how to feel
and not to feel
in a world of endless injustices
is stupid
The internet is both a wondrous and idiotic place
sometimes, often both
Step outside of your bubble

What you perceive in theory
and especially on-line (see: here)
is not always the same thing in practice

i.e., real life
In fact, it's often the opposite
But you don't learn that
if you never travel outside of your own bubble, kids
There's numerous examples of this
on here, many of which get ridiculed
but they're pretty dead on.
Life in your mind?
Not the same thing as life on the block
And your block?
Wholly different than someone else's
especially somewhere else
You can nuance all you want online
and theorize and craft and even practice...digitally
But the stark reality many of you will face one day
is that
shit ain't like that.

5

This place often feels like a secret support group
for battered and abused people
who want to escape reality
and create their own rules and language
It's therapy
and this is a couch
with ads
And that's fine except that I see
far too many people mistaking *this* for reality
It's not
Reality sucks
Life is short
and hard
You gotta take your joy where you can get it and endure the rest
Take care of your own
Survival of the fittest, folks
it's a thing
Booooooooootstrapsssssss!
Nature, after all
could give a fuck about tumblr.

Anyway, this is an i'm-too-old-for-tumblr-bitter-old-man poem
but take it for what it's worth
A million "likes" or "winning" an argument online
means jack shit on the street

I'd like to wake up one morning
and read the news from somewhere
anywhere
that isn't corporately owned
sponsored by bullshit
secretly encoded in SEO
stupid on purpose
snarky
racist
bigoted
asinine
or slathered in sarcasm
from people too bitter and brainwashed
to admit that they are merely lonely and attention seeking
whores
in this slave new world

6

Social media is the Ipecac for human opinion
It still puzzles me why everyone feels so compelled
to puke their every whim
every second of the day
completely unprovoked
and uncompensated for
Just barf, everywhere
And I say this because I come from
several eras where this was not so
and struggle to remember what it was
that we did then
that was comparable

I am sick of identity politics!
I'm sick of the race card
I'm sick of every goddamn conversation

turning into a witch hunt
All of this shit online
is like a never ending soap opera
with extra commercials and it's gag-inducing
To quote Phil Collins:
I don't care anymore!
I know who I am
That's all that matters to me
Everyone else?
You do you
I invoke the 69th Amendment,
which says:
In cases of extreme bullshit/hypocrisy
(see: year 2015)
the right to bear Phil Collins is granted

Listening to old and uncensored Sam Kinison clips
on the radio
makes me realize just how out of place I am
here in 2015
Maybe I am a dinosaur
Maybe I am "dusty"
It's a weird feeling
because I grew up listening to those monologues
and drank them in like water
Sam couldn't get away with that kind of stuff now
No one can
Not without an apology tour
or shining Ice Cube's shoes
after he scolds you for using a word
he was chiefly responsible
for encouraging white America to use!
To express yourself freely
in today's thought crime
powder keg society
is to play with matches
lest you be labeled with the scarlet letter N
of "Nazism"
But I play with matches just the same
flicking them one by one

down into the sewer
of the web
where they will collect and mix with all the other things
no one speaks about in real-life language
because no speak is the newspeak
everything is taboo
and racist
and sexist
and transphobic
and misogynistic
and Islamophobic
and so on
and someday everything will burn
and someday there will be no more language
and someday there will be no more us
and someday there will no more earth
and someday the universe will let out a sigh of relief

the independence day that never comes

I often wonder if
one day
some far off distant day from right now
if we last long enough
to have a common enemy
of the entire planet
if that would finally unite us
together
as a species
and make everyone forget their bigotry
for just one day

Probably not

Our species never evolved
beyond territorial pissings
I suspect we will take that with us
to the grave
and beyond

Planet earth was not destroyed by communism after all,
but by semantics

hashtag buy stuff, hashtag shut the fuck up and die

Did the daily celebrations of consumerism
start before The Matrix took over
or after?
I can't remember any more

Happy National [WHATEVER! JUST BUY STUFF ALREADY!] Day!

I'm not gonna talk about how the pointless
the mass BLIND celebration
of killing each other
is one of the most ridiculous things of all-time
for the human species to do
collectively
Nor am I gonna mention the hypocrisy in doing so
in the face of perpetual war
both abroad and on the home front
Nope
It's just another Monday
and goddamn the cacophony is loud today
so, shut the fuck up and go buy stuff already, asshole
there's a war on,
and everyone must do their part
buy, buy, buy!

Raze your consciousness
Never woke
but slept
inept
hit that snooze
lose
let go
Obey
Consume
Sleep
Buy
Hashtag
Die

2015

War is not peace
Freedom is not slavery
Ignorance is not strength
Compliance is not revolution
Inclusion is not acceptance
Losing is not winning
Symbols are not systems
Illusion is not self

librarian's creed

This is my library. There are many like it, but this one is mine.

My library is my best friend. It is my life. I must master it as I must master my life.

My library, without me, is useless. Without my library, I am useless. I must use my library true. I must read better than my enemy who is trying to outsmart me. I must read about him before he reads about me. I will...

My library and myself know that what counts in this war is not the shows we watch, the noise on the radio, or the buzz online. We know that it is the books that count. We will read...

Before God, I swear this creed. My library and myself are the defenders of my country. We are the masters of our enemy. We are the saviors of my life.

So be it, until ignorance is conquered and there is no illiteracy, but knowledge!

the vultures of hotel florida

Today I watched a group of vultures camp out in a tree
hanging over a freshly killed dog/deer/carcass
They set up shop fairly quickly and spent the entire day
picking the animal's bones while the flies danced their dance
and planted seeds of freshly birthed maggot eggs inside

Even now, in the torrential daily downpour
the vultures wait it out
they are perched on thick wet branches
in the great green inferno
savoring the flavor
still on their blood-soaked beaks

This immediately reminded me of the media
The only difference is that vultures
don't shove microphones and cameras
down relatives of the deceased's throats
while they chew on the innards and smack their gums and ask:
How does it feeeeeeeeeeeeeeeeeeeeeeeeeeeeeeeelllllllll?

The vultures, like the media
still cleaning the carcasses
know not to let anything go to waste
the same as any local news anchor
who also like to chew on innards
and smack their gums
before they wipe their their blood-soaked beaks

This is the cycle of death
here in the land of rape and honey
No rebirth,
just death, dismemberment
and digestion
BURP
This, here, in the year of our Lord
two thousand and fifteen
here in AmeriKKKa

[please stand by for a message from our sponsors]

what does the billboard say?

Come and play
come and play
forget about the Movement
remember that?
I do

When Zach "I forgot who I am" De La Rocha
preached this
few listened
fewer understood
the entertainment and news industries did
they excelled at getting people to play
like right now
where people tear each other apart
in the middle of the street
on live TV
with ads
Oh, but it's just entertainment!
Uh huh.
Go buy some fuckin' soap
Go buy some more fuckin' dick pills
you slob!
To quote Furious Styles:
They want us to kill ourselves
Why is it that there's a gun shop
on almost every corner
in the fucked up part of town, USA?
The same reason there is
a liquor store on almost every corner
in fuckup town, USA
Why?
They want us to kill ourselves
Literally
figuratively
spiritually
But first!
They want your money!
As long as they make a profit

color no longer matters
unless it's green
by any means necessary?
Yes...
by whatever means
you can empty
your pockets

[After these messages, we'll be right back]

the end is nigh (an ode to political season)

I don't have to agree with you to like you
nor like you to agree with you
I also don't have to like you to respect you
but I sure as hell can't like you
if I don't respect you
and respect is earned, asshole

Summer is ready to burn hot
everything will be on fire soon
even you
leaving nothing but ashes

By the time November rolls around
we'll all be crispy critters
walking scorched earth
and complaining constantly
because everyone is always right
clutching for the same old straws
with charred hands
You ain't seen nothin' yet

fuck me for your service

I've been meaning to write about why we are pressured
no, brainwashed
into automatically thanking the military
or any US military member, from any era
from anywhere, for that matter
for "their service"
It drives me nuts
Public schools ask make children to do this now
It's expected
And goddamnit, you better comply, mister!
lest you risk being labeled a socialist, a communist or a queer!
You're supposed to drop whatever you're doing and say:
THANK YOU FOR YOUR SERVICE SIR!
And then get down on your knees are start polishing the next deco-
rated cock you see
until it shines like a mirror
Why don't we do this shtick with public school teachers?
Or nurses?
Firefighters?
Complete strangers will walk up to soldiers everywhere
and thank them (lick them)
for their service to their country
they slobber on them like that for an eternity
and I end up feeling embarrassed for the soldier
who ends up drenched in saliva and cum
I often feel like butting in and asking:
what EXACTLY is it that you did again
and why are we thanking you for it...?
But with my luck, I'll get the guy with the crew cut, no neck
and the tomato-red face screaming at me
with little bits of hot flaming spittle
spewing from the corners of his mouth
lighting things on fire:

"PROTECTING YOUR FREEEEEEEEEEEEEDOM YOU COMMU-
NIST COCKSUCKER PINKO FAIRY FAGGOT PIECE OF JESUS
HATING SHEEEEEEITTTTTTTTTT!!!!!!!"

But no
I mean, really...NO
This kind of brainwashing has gone on long enough
and there's no end in sight
I honestly don't get it
who started this trend?
It reminds me of people saying 'Bless You'
when someone sneezes
there's no logic in it
yet no one questions it
Someone please explain to me why it is
we are pressured
to thank these young men and women
and what it is we are thanking them for?
spare me the FOX News version
I am most grateful for your explanation and I will pack a lunch
I have both friends and family members
who have served proudly
(their words)
and I never once sucked any of their dicks for it
nor did they ask me to
But what the fuck do I know?
Thank you for helping to kill all those Iraqis?
Thanks for blowing up a grandma in Pakistan?
Thanks for the never ending blood storm in Afghanistan?
Thanks for the illegal torture and captivity at Gitmo?
Thanks for perpetual war?
Help me out here

bad news is the new heroin, so shoot up, buttercup

Is racist white America fascinated by black vernacular speech
and how "people of color" talk in private spaces
or are the coloreds paranoid and frothing at the mouth in a prison
of their own creation?
On the next Maury!

This dilemma reminds me of Richard
"nopal en la frente"
Rodriguez and his incessant whining
on the pages of his famous book
which is in every forced "Hispanic" section
in every bookstore in America
In it, he laments about the loss of his private language
in so-called White spaces
It also makes me think of Quentin Tarantino
and any number of people these days
who treat Black and Brown culture as a fetish
I also find it interesting
how everyone now views George Zimmerman
as White
It wasn't that long ago
that people were citing his so-called Peruvian heritage
as some kind of qualifier
for not being a racist dickhead
Hell, there were even "latino" websites defending him
at one point
here in the twilight zone
but now that the tables have turned,
not a peep from them defending him anymore
How convenient
And here we all are,
in the middle of this racial cluster fuck
in the US capital of cluster fucks (see: Florida)
and all anyone wants is more
More!
Mas!
MOOOOOORE
Zimmerman is now White,
officially, mind you

adopted by seething bigots and hate-filled hypocrites,
who would be just as happy
were the strange fruit a gross domestic product
and I'm sure Georgie is more than okay with that
seeing as how they paid him a large sum of money
and continue to defend him
at every turn
despite his obvious Brown "handicap"
Yet, Obama is always Black,
despite his White mother
Funny how that works
Even Black people see Obama as Black-only
because perception is reality now

I keep saying to myself
that we live in unprecedented times
and in many ways we do
But the more things change...
well, you know the rest
Onward, backwards!
Round and round we go
Countdown to oblivion
The bacteria and microscopic lifeforms
that take over the planet when we're gone
will breathe a heavy sigh of relief after we're all dead
"Whew! Glad that's over with!"

You want to know what's funny?
The news doesn't report the news anymore
I realize that's hardly news
but it's true!
What they do report is 24-hours of constant garbage,
hell-bent on inciting fear and loathing
in every viewer and listener
They want you to hate your neighbor,
hate yourself and hate the world
but they also want you to be a loyal consumer
and to buy the products they market
during commercial breaks
Burn your city to ashes
but please stay tuned for these messages!

"Put the gun down and check out this new toothpaste! It'll get your
teeth whiter than Paula Deen's sheets!"

I watched all the major news networks
on Saturday morning
they all ran the same stories over and over again
They all debated Paula Deen,
they all lamented the George Zimmerman trial
they all balked at the weather
And that was it
On every single channel
the same stories cropped up again and again
with different plastic-looking people vomiting out tidbits
about this or that
while smiling and wiping their mouths
after they spewed out the so-called news,
then they started selling things.
Rinse, repeat

"And now....horkkkk! gahhhhhh!!!!!...a word from our sponsor!"

I used to read National Geographic
So what, right?
Right
But I'll be damned if I wasn't floored every time I read it
because of some amazing new discovery or development
that the national media wouldn't touch with a 10-foot pole
And that's what gets me
There's a lot of stuff going on
amazing things
hell, positive and mind-blowing things
but you'll never hear about them
unless you seek them out from independent sources
because They want you to stand in traffic
They want you to burn your neighborhood down
They want you to beat each other in the skull
and scoop each other's brains out and into your mouths
but more than anything
They want your money and your attention
The national media is not in the business
of informing anyone of anything

They are in the business of selling products
and keeping people as fearful and hate-filled as possible
Why?
So you keep tuning in!
Don't believe me?
Watch the national news for an hour
see if your blood pressure doesn't shoot through the roof
and you're not left clawing your eyeballs out
feeling as if the world is ending
one news segment at a time
And maybe it is!
But fuck if there's not other things,
positive things,
happening on this flaming ball of water

There's an agenda here
It's been going on for a long time
We have allowed the government and the media
to paralyze us all with fear
so that they can keep pushing the envelope further and further
Fear and loathing!

"We'll keep you safe! Just grant us the power, by any means neces-
sary! Sit back, relax and have another cold one. We'll take it from
here! Right after these messages! You betcha!"
Open your tablet,
 turn on the television,
read your phone
or god forbid,
buy and read an actual print post newspaper,
all you're going to find is death, destruction, hate and fear

I sincerely believe now
that so many of us
are addicted to glorified tragedy
viral news cycles
twisting along the digital plains
like tornadoes in KS
sucking us up like so many rubes
and spitting us back out no wiser
definitely dumber

we're like junkies
suckin' dick for
the next fix
Death and destruction,
blood and guts
tears and pain
gimme sorrow
gimme tears
gimme grieving families and
bodies floating down the river
halleluiah!
Gimme fire!
Gimme, gimme, gimme!
What's the scoop!
What's the score here?
My soul
for another juicy, raw, blood-soaked story, please
to go!

We must have that next hit
and we must have it now
before the rush is even over
it becomes old news
and we are again searching for the next fix,
the next latest,
greatest thing
the sacrifice
the tar on the spoon
the rush up the bloodstream
into our rotting brains
Mmmmmm...yeah,
that's the stuff.
Ahhhhhh...
Bad news is the new heroin
The media are the new dealers
Welcome to the real drug war

targeted killing in the age of hope and change

A lawful killing
in self-defense
is not an assassination
or so They say

In Big Brother's view:

"a lethal operation conducted against a U.S. citizen whose conduct
poses an imminent threat of violent attack against the United States
would be a legitimate act of national self-defense"

A legitimate act of national self-defense
as defined by those
with the guns
and the legal recourse required
to murder you with

by any other name
is still a rose as true
as the blood spatter
upon its white pedals
outside the book depository
one sunny morning
just ask:

JFK,
RFK,
MLK,
Malcolm X,
Ruben Salazar,
Gary Webb
and countless other
Americans
who posted a threat
to the status quo
because the use of lethal force,
used by the Blue Gang or
the Red Gang

consistent with the laws of war
against any individual
who is a legitimate military target
would be lawful
in the eyes of those
who fill lobby coffers
as thoughtlessly as they
fill pine coffins
with acts of
patriotism and national defense

merchandise no. 5

I'd like to buy the world a [REDACTED]
which is delicious and refreshing
and good to the last drop
the only thing like [REDACTED]
is [REDACTED]
where there's [OBEY] there's hospitality
along the highway to anywhere
what you want is a [REDACTED]
but just so you know
don't ever ask any questions about
Merchandise No. 5
or you will end up like Gary Webb
two bullet holes
in the back of your head
and a suicide note
that says:
Have a [OBEY]
and a smile!

KNOW. YOUR. HISTORY.
But remember to refresh yourself
six million times a day
with [REDACTED]!
It's pure as sunlight and
the best friend [REDACTED] ever had
The [REDACTED] we know today
still contains [OBEY]
Because you can't beat the real thing!
To make it real,
the [SLEEP] is removed
and after that,
life tastes good
Perfecting that extraction took until 1929
before that there were still
trace amounts
of [CONSUME]'s psychoactive elements in
the real thing

Today, the extraction is done
at a chemical processing facility
in New Jersey
by a company called [REDACTED]
In 2003, [CONSUME] imported
175,000 kilograms of [DO NOT QUESTION]
for [AUTHORITY]
That's enough to make more than
$200 million worth of
Ice cold sunshine

Connect the dots and
open happiness!
the cold, crisp taste of [SLEEP]
is only achieved through the importation
of illegal vegetation
to the plantation nation
where the overseers of
[OBEY] reap profits from the third world
making billions of dollars
because you can't beat the real thing, sucker

Because the official [REDACTED] of summer
is a sign of good taste
Look up, AmeriKKKa!
Do not pass Go
And go directly to jail
if you try the [SLEEP] side of life
you get stigmatized for generations
or end up dead
but never mind that
Merchandise No. 5
is guarded
by armed men
who know that
whoever you are
whatever you do
wherever you may be
when you think of refreshment
think of ice cold [REDACTED]!

Enjoy!
Make it real
Catch the wave for [DO NOT QUESTION]
Open happiness.
It's always
Red, white and you.

drone on the range

Drone, drone on the range
where the fear and the apathy roam
where seldom is heard
an encouraging word
y los Mexicanos
die every day

Drone, drone on the range!
where the Brown and Black people play
where seldom is heard,
and encouraging word
and the skies are filled
with killers
all day

I'm a little teacup
short and stout
here's my drone
here's my scout

40,000 more border agents,
Mr. President
costs $50 billion more dollars
700 miles of double-layered fence
488 video surveillance systems
6 VADER radar systems
18 Drones
15 Blackhawk helicopters
along the new Barrio-Berlin wall
radar surveillance and
military tactics

similar to what is being used in Iraq and Afghanistan
similar to what is being used in Iraq and Afghanistan
similar to what is being used in Iraq and Afghanistan
similar to what is being used in Iraq and Afghanistan
similar to what is being used in Iraq and Afghanistan
similar to what is being used in Iraq and Afghanistan

similar to what is being used in Iraq and Afghanistan
similar to what is being used in Iraq and Afghanistan
similar to what is being used in Iraq and Afghanistan
similar to what is being used in Iraq and Afghanistan
similar to what is being used in Iraq and Afghanistan
similar to what is being used in Iraq and Afghanistan

Hope and Change though!
Can a brother get a refund?

this is some gourmet shit!

I can smell a politician a mile away
That politician you voted for?
You know the one
They fucking stink
They're rancid
like so many
landfills teeming
with opinions and maggots
(which are the same thing)
from eras past

There's people out here
sewin' their oats
in your backyard and mine
on the street corner
of 15 minute Avenue
sellin' shit sandwiches
and calling it "activism"
Okay, hoss!
You gonna put some mustard
on that there caca panini you're hawkin me?
Shit all smells the same
no matter how many pieces of cheese
you put on it, kids
You say a side of potato salad?
I say a loving spoonful of horseshit
politricks and marketing
and propaganda
but, lawd, people are hungry
these days!
starving even
they line the streets of this
giant playpen
we call a nation
and they all wet themselves
waiting for change
and hope!
and to be spoon-fed a mouthful

of the gourmet shit
served up by guvmint

Bon Appétit, mother fucker

the in-house drive-by strikes back

Funny!
HAWHAW!
how you can now
witness something LIVE!
on the TEEVEE
and social media
social slime
thought crime
national pastime
hit re-wind <<
document it,
photograph it,
record it,
capture it
fuck it
smack it up
flip it
rub it down
oh, no!
and bear witness to it
all under the supervision
of Gawd almighty
and the NSA
all as it happens

LIVE!
FUCK IT! WE'LL DO IT LIVE!
FUCKIN THING...SUCKS!

and people will still believe
whatever it is
which suits their own personal narrative
uninformed
spun
skewed
distorted
and pushed through so many filters
like shit out your candy ass

into the john
talking heads
pundits and prophets
walking dead
twitter faggots and sockets
YouTube personalities
Subscribe!
and more "threads" than you can
shake a hashtag at, Jack
lies/propaganda
and outright bullshit,
especially when it comes to
the three wise men:
the mainstream media,
the corporations (who are really people)
and the government

We really are all just victims!
here in Victimland!
asking our daily bread
our daily brainwash
and our daily dose
of the in-house drive-by

Bang.

blue pills

It's a federal crime
to cut the cables
that feed the world wide web
into our thick skulls
but we should do it anyway
hell, it might even be an international crime
and possibly a "hate crime" at this point
warranting death
via public shaming
and change dot org petitions
on a live stream near you
It gets tiring screaming
on a daily basis
about the hypocrisies and outright crimes
of the current administration
in an attempt to rally the troops
because as we all know
most people don't really care
Sure, sure...
we Tweet about it
make memes about injustices
put em up on IG
we pontificate
gnash our teeth
wring our little hands
and then sigh
we RT it and then forget about it
sound about right?

I mean, if we're settling for daily mass shootings and cops shooting
up innocent bystanders just because they're mad, well, fuck...might
as well take the mother fuckin' red pill.
It's all Wonderland anyway, right..?
except that the story never really ends

we wake up in our beds
and believe whatever we want to believe
Cops shooting citizens to hunt cops who shoot citizens...brilliant

You take the blue pill, the story ends. You wake up in your bed and believe whatever you want to believe.

You take the red pill, you stay in Wonderland, and I show you how deep the rabbit hole goes.

And buddy, it is fuckin' DEEP

knives and guns and gang fights in the age of hope and change

I really despise that if you're critical of empire now you get demon-ized by the left but if you criticize the right you get lumped in the with people on the left who won't criticize empire...

This is bullshit.

And then you have the crazy people, on both sides who swear up and down that it's all his fault/not his fault at all. It's their fault! It's our fault! It's nobody's fault! Yet no one is ever held accountable. How's the political process supposed to work again..?

You have the lunatics on the right who freak out about everything BUT what's really wrong, and the infants on the left who turn their backs on everything and suck their thumbs in the corner.

"It's better than the alternative..."

Fuck this guy! The left would be clawing their eyeballs out were W. still in office and doing the exact same things. But somehow, here in Bizarro World, everyone wants to pretend that things are just super. Or that it's the last days.

And it's all a goddamn broken record falling on deaf ears, in a dark room with a blind man looking for a black cat that ain't even there. Everyone knows this shit but no one cares. I keep waiting for that one "thing" that'll wake people up but it never happens. We just keep sinking further into apathy and waiting for the NFL season to start, perpetually.

It drives me nuts watching this weird, wacky upside down clus-ter-fuck that everyone pretends there's nothing we can do about.

Those who were anti-establishment not too long ago are now pro-establishment. Those who were pro-establishment not too long ago are now anti-establishment.

!!! Huh?

And for what?? To defend your team? Your colors? Your gang? Blue vs. Red, go team go! 'Merica! Love it or leave it, asshole!

Unreal.

You're right. Hang on, Charlie Brown, I think I see Lucy holding the football again...

amnesia is fun

No one remembers that war
Or its casualties
Amnesia is fun
No one remembers the other wars either
There's one been going on now for
12 years?
More?
I forget too
But everyone remembers great speeches
Can't wait for the one on Tuesday
Doesn't matter what he says
Just as long as it makes us feeeeeeel good
Maybe he'll lip sync it
Because in 2013
We're all about appearances
Substance is so
old school

nobody's listening

So much to rant about
but ain't nobody really listening
Feels futile
today anyway
I'm not in favor
of banning guns
I'm not in favor of
putting guns in schools either
Clowns to the left of me
Jokers to the right
Here I am
Oh!
And Quentin Tarantino was dropping N-bombs
at the golden globes last night
Color me: shocked
He won an award
This film will be his highest grossing film
ever

The End.

nothing to see here

The police do not want citizens recording them
The police do not want the media recording them
The police will police themselves
The police will replace the media
in all instances of broken law,
broken bones
and broken homes

The police will disperse accurate
reliable and timely information
in accordance with the standards
we have come to expect from them

The police will not be subjected to your scrutiny
The police will not be under the watch of the anyone's eye
The police have their own
and it is watching you,
right now

The police will replace your local politicians
The police will tell you what you can eat
where you can shit
and what is safe to read
The police will decide who's life matters
The police will be judge
jury and executioner
No one is above the law
except the police

The police know what's best for the populace
The police do not require transparency
The police would never try to cover anything up
The police are not in the business
of controlling information
The police
are
in
control

Carry on, citizen

NOTHING TO SEE HERE
LITERALLY

perception is reality

Mental illness

[they have many code words for this these days; liberalism, conservatism, socialism, communism, anarchism, couch potatoism, jingoism, deathism, capitalism, cathoderayism, selfieism]

comes in all shapes and sizes and it's not always easy to detect but you know it when you see it. Sometimes it's blatant and other times it's hidden. Sanity is what we tell each other it is and is really just a game of numbers

[1,9, 8, 4,...]

- the sane outnumber the insane so what we define as "sane" is only a matter of more of us than them.

More importantly, how do we define it? Insanity is defined as a violation of societal norms.

[Well now...how many of those so-called violations can we count on each hand? Hmmm? Seems like more every day yet we all salivate for more. More death, more violence, more chaos, mooorrreee football, mooorrreeee Amerikkkan idol, more, more, more, whore, whore...]

The word "sane" is derived from the Latin "sanus", meaning "healthy" – therefore to be "insane" is to be unhealthy and so on, which is to say that you may have "poor" mental health.

[And we all know that poor = bad in this slave new world, yeah? Poor...eradicate the poor - stick them in the fire to keep the wealthy warm. Eat the poor, fuck the poor, destroy the poor!]

I've met a whole lot of crazy people in my professional life and a few in my personal one – no two are alike.

I once asked a guy who worked at a mental institution, what qualifications does a person need to do his job. His answer? Be a good wrestler. I laughed nervously in response, he did not.

Metal institutions are interesting places,

[perception is reality]

they are usually devoid of stimuli and yet you can sense that violence can break out at any time.

[like now]

Unlike a prison, the people confined at mental institutions are regularly released back into society for another swing at sanity.

[your hell is another's heaven]

Anyway, as the world spins off of its axis with crazy people finally becoming the majority population on earth, all I can think about it Edward Munch's "The Scream".

[one's scream is another's delight]

To you it may look like a tortured soul but to the idiocracy it may very well be a person overcome with joy at the second coming of their savior.

[Who knows? I guess we'll all find out one day]

Are we all fuckin' nuts or just misunderstood? Only one way to find out.

[long live the new flesh]

pissing contest

It is fascinating
how on some days
when the french fries are just right
(and maybe you've asked the kid behind the counter not to spit on
your order)
the collective fast food nation
that is,
we of the Sitcom Republic
host to the Super Bowl of politricks and polidicks,
we will celebrate a person's death one day
and then abhor it the next
(context matters of course, you say!)
but we seem to be collectively schizophrenic about dying,
death and the dead
and urinating on the dead

I guess because we expect more
of our brainwashed teenagers
who murder people for paychecks and commercialized glory
Is it real or is it Memorex?
I mean
do we cheer a guy's body being dragged through the streets
and then 'boo' when they pee on him?
Boooooo!!
when just yesterday
we called for an end to the death penalty?
Not the same thing you say...
that guy deserved it you say
but not this guy...
Ok!

Head shots and glamour shots
they all make the news
the dirty laundry,
if it bleeds it leads
Is it a question of:
he/she deserved it...?
or a question of execution is wrong in all cases

different names, different places
different expressions on their faces
I honestly don't think anyone knows anymore
but urinating on the dead is bad
got it

(note to self: OK to kill them, maim them, torture them, detain
them, just don't piss on the enemy. And for fuck's sake! Don't pose
with the dead after you've killed AND pissed on them!)
It'll be old news next week anyway
and we will still be spinning it
justifying it
condemning it
forgetting it
and pissing on it
these are all chess moves anyway
It's your move
and please,
try to hit the target this time.

are you ready for some football?!

FADE IN:

Tom Brokaw stares into the camera while off-camera we hear his producers yelling at him:

Get on with it, Tom! Let's go!

Tom shakes his head with regret and reaches for a bottle of Jack Daniels. The brown liquor splashes down his face and onto to his sport jacket as he drinks greedily and then throws the bottle off camera.

CRASH

Tom reaches under the desk and reveals a large caliber hand gun.

He points the gun at his own head and says:

*This **IS** the news!!*

The screen flashes a SCRAMBLED SIGNAL and we hear the sound of STATIC then the INDIAN HEAD test pattern is shown.
A GUNSHOT is heard with people SCREAMING in the background.

Tom, No!!!!!

CUT TO:

I'm still reeling over the execution video that was circulating yesterday. It made little "news". But that's not surprising is it? In it, two guys (Mx. cartel members, also uncle and nephew) state their names and what they did and then they are brutally executed while the camera rolls.

CUT TO:

One guy has his head sawed off with a chainsaw and the other guy has his throat slit. The masked executioner then proceeds to hack his head off with a large knife. It takes him a long time to complete the task and when he does, he places the head on the body only to watch it roll off on to the ground.

These guys are extremely calm about the entire situation. They offer no protest, they don't scream or yell. The nephew watches his uncle get his head sawed off and doesn't flinch, even with blood all over him - he simply waits his turn.

CUT TO:

Every other day stories like this creep into the various social media outlets and people either IGNORE THEM, recoil in horror or nervously crack jokes.

"Won't be going there for vacation! Hahahahahaha!"

As if what is happening is not real.

As if it is occurring on the moon.

As if it is all a drama sponsored by beer companies and endorsed by people with stock in private prisons, the military and google.

CUT TO:

I only commit this to memory because it is surreal to switch channels from Monday Night Football - obscenely decorated with caricatures of so-called Hispanic heritage month - to the brutality/reality of the war on drugs destroying Mexico from the inside out.

And we all watch it while scratching ourselves, eating popcorn and guzzling lite beer.

CUT TO:

Hank Williams, sunglasses off, sings:

Estas listo para el futbol?!

Suddenly Hank's head is sawed off with a chainsaw. BZZZZZZZZZZ ZZZZZZZZTTTTTTTTTTTTTTTTTTTTTT

Mexican-themed confetti vomits all over the screen.

The head rolls on the astro turf where a Dallas Cowboy kicks it off screen and it goes flying through the uprights.

Jerry Jones smiles and claps his hands.

CUT TO:

Tony Romo sacked, wincing in pain.

CUT TO:

Extreme close-up of two men beheaded
(sinister laughter in the background)

CUT TO:

Mariachi band singing

CUT TO:

Sexy shampoo ad

CUT TO:

'Feel good' fast food ad

CUT TO:

Political ad condemning "illegals"

CUT TO:

Insurance ad with geckos in sombreros.

CUT TO:

WIDE ANGLE: football fans in 'war paint' screaming for blood

Are YOU ready for some football??

FADE TO BLACK

killing the messenger

Sometimes, when you dig deep enough
people are kind and write suicide notes
so that you don't have to
And you get not one
but two bullet holes in the head
in the wake of what they will say was depression
Because dead men know all too well
that when you find yourself covered in enough dirt
someone always comes looking to fill in the holes
Left by those who would rather
die standing on two feet
than survive kneeling on a rotting body of lies
And though the news would rather spin a tale
of government assassination as something new under the sun
but dead men with stories to tell know better
stories of desert drones with corporate loans
of magic bullets and liars pulpits
stories with code name killings and Faux news cheering
stories from the Audubon Ballroom
stories from the Ambassador Hotel
stories from the Silver Dollar Bar
stories from the Lorraine Motel
stories of CIA conspiracies, crack cocaine and secret wars
stories live from Georgia's death row, justice nevermore
And so they preach that the truth will set you free
if sometimes that freedom means death and a last minute plea
for the killing of the messenger
lets everyone sleep better at night in the united states
of deaf, dumb and blind
where convenience rules and no one minds
a little lie, a giant lie, an endless lie
it's all the same
here where the dark alliances control the game

once upon a time

Once Upon A Time...
The United States of AmeriKKKa
Dropped a bad guy into the ocean blue
And everyone lived happily ever after
The End.

only here

Only here can you murder someone in cold blood, wash your hands in it and get rewarded, with cash, by sympathetic bigots and television networks.

Only here can you turn a miscarriage of justice into a publicity stunt and smile into the camera with sickly eyes and jagged teeth while declaring that it was "the will of Gawd."

Only here can you pull the trigger on camera and have it endorsed by soap, toothpaste and cheeseburgers.

Only here do we quietly fume while obediently fulfilling our corporate master's wishes.

Only here can you paint with the blood of your murder victims and their family's tears and become rich by selling your "art" to vampires, ghouls and the living dead.

Only here can you bankroll your future by riding the publicity whore train to keep your name in the headlines and further cash in on the blood of young Black boys and Brown girls.

Only here do we tolerate injustice and match it with apathy and virtual beaches where we quietly stick our heads in the sand and wait for the bad man to get what he came for and go away.

Only here are we all simultaneously victims and villains.

Only here will we usher in the apocalypse with coffee, hashtags, selfies and memes.

Whatever the people with bumper stickers, microphones, flags and signs are fighting to "take back" never left.

Only here.

we win yet?

So.............

How's the war on terror going?

We win yet..?

Just checking.

Since, yanno,
no one fucking talks about it
at all, ever,
in any way whatsoever.
We just keep on goin',
mindlessly hoping it'll all just go awaaaaaaay...

This is such a bizarre fucking time to be alive.

after the internet

My god how 9/11 affected the lot of us.
And the funny thing is,
all these years later,
those individual stories will never be told,
much less understood,
because they are buried under both the remains of the dead
and the various narratives that those who write history
would have us believe.
Or snark,
apathy and the misgivings of children
too young to comprehend what life was like
prior to the birth of George Orwell's work
come to life.

The ramifications will not be understood
for decades and even then I'm not sure
anyone will care.
But goddamn if everything didn't tip upside down
that day
and forever after until we unraveled into this...
this thing - this existence,
if you can call it that.
What we resemble now
is less like a human existence
and more like a situational comedy
produced by robots
with endless robot sponsors
and an ocean of robotic consumers.

We are dead inside.
We are ugly outside.
What comes next?
What happens after the Internet?

I'm almost afraid to ask.

side effects of drugs advertised on tv

The drugs that you pop in your mouth
in between the dull hours of your menial existence
have side effects
I know you've heard them
A nice man or woman can often be heard
Explaining these things to you during the commercial breaks

These drugs:

Might kill you
May cause suicidal ideations
Your dick might fall off
You may grow a third tit
You might cut your mother's head off
and make it a birthday cake
which you may take a huge shit on
Can cause diabetes, cancer, heart disease, Ebola
May cause gay, crazy NAZI AIDS
You might piss your pants in public
You could possibly shit yourself while ordering eggs at Denny's at
3:00 p.m. on a Sunday
Your grandparents will instantly know what you masturbate to
Might possibly cause a hard-on, even after death

But wait, there's more!

The side effects of pot, which is still illegal in lots of places are:

Happiness
Sleepiness
Increased Appetite
Mellow attitude or euphoria, depending on strain
Cures everything
Grows everywhere

dnc 2016 opening speech

There is nothing wrong with your smart phone
Do not attempt to adjust the Wi-Fi
We are controlling transmission
If we wish to make it louder
we will bring up the volume
If we wish to make it softer
we will tune it to a whisper
We will control the resolution
We will control the stream
We can enhance the image
make it transmit our thoughts
140 characters at a time
to your consumer minds
We can change the focus to a soft blur
or sharpen it to High Definition
For the next lifetime
sit quietly
do not think
and we will control all that you see and hear
We repeat: there is nothing wrong
with your smart phone
You are about to participate
in a great adventure
You are about to experience
the shock and awe
of the Marketing Propaganda Industrial Complex
which reaches from the trending hashtags
to the viral videos
We are in control
Do not question
Do not resist
Obey

FIVE

more demons

For a short period of time
in my 20s
in the midst of the fog of 1,000 drunken nights
while both soaked with alcohol and stained with nictone
I borrowed the eye of God
and for the first time
I saw everyone as they were intended to be seen
either as demons
or as human beings
there were no angels
because all the angels were dead
and I could finally see why none of them ever
answered any prayers
least of all mine,
which were simply to not be so lonely,
get laid and be "discovered"
whatever the fuck that meant

These sexless angel corpses were everywhere
their bodies piled high to the heavens,
which were on fire
as chunks of Holy City fell to the ground
and the whole scene looked
like something out of a Nazi death camp

The demons, however, tried to blend in
just as they do now
by wearing human skin
like a cheap suit
upon their deformed shapes
some looked better than others
but imagine a rather large demonic figure
clad with horns and teeth and scars and hooves
claws and wings
trying to stretch into the skin of a man
like a latex glove pulled over the antlers of a murdered deer
I could only see these things
with the eye of God

whom I was sure was dead
but everywhere I went I saw them
these talking skin suits
laughing, drinking, playing, fucking
and feasting upon unsuspecting human beings
in public places
eating the remains of the angels
and fucking the dead
while reveling in their sin
as this was truly Hell on earth
or so I thought

Much to the chagrin of my friends,
who thought I was out of my fucking mind
and on drugs
(I was)
I would try and point these things out
in public places,
like the pool hall,
the club
the john
but none of them ever saw what I saw
And then one day one of them saw me

I have been blind ever since.

don't answer the goddamn phone!

If every time you sleep you dream of a ringing phone
and every dream you let it ring and ring
what does that say about you?
What if you shoot the phone?
What if it keeps ringing, even after you shoot it
with a strangled and warped tone?
Mocking you
I wonder:
If a phone rings in your dream,
do you answer it?
Who's on the other end?
You?
Or something else entirely?
Do younger people dream of cell phones only?
Do they text?
Sext?
And do older folks dream of land lines,
pay phones and back and white telephone wires?
Who calls you?
in your dream?
I'm asking
Who has been calling me for the last 40 years?
Why do I never pick up?
I think I know why.
I think I can shoot the phone as many times as I like.
Light it on fire, smash it to pieces
and throw it to the bottom of the ocean
still it rings.
And it will keep on ringing
until it doesn't.
Until I answer it.

gawd

What if god was one of us..?
Haha! Fuck that song!
No, but really...
what if god was homeless?
a drifter...
begging for money in the streets
sucking cock
sleeping under the bridge
he's dirty
he smells
and he has a host of mental illnesses
from years of people misinterpreting things he said
He drinks a lot
and most of the time people pretend
he isn't even there
there is much speculation
on how he came to lose everything

You most likely would not recognize the guy
He's been through two bitter divorces
and his children refuse to keep in touch
he had a steady job for a little while
as a Wal-Mart greeter in Texas
but he was fired for wearing a religious button on his vest
Now he spends his days at the public library
trying to bathe in the bathroom
and working on his blog
Tweeting to no one.
Doing it for the Gram.

what the 90s were like

It was cruising down the Boulevard
until your pager goes off and then finding a payphone
to get the address to the house party

It was getting pulled over on Lincoln and
having a parade of pigs pull out their guns and trashing your car
and telling you to get the fuck out of town
or else

it was rolling up on the party where
you would get fuckin' wasted outta your goddamn gourd, smoking
mota, talking shit and then getting jumped into the clique by the
homies outside before pounding another 40

It was fucking a firme hyna on the floor and ending up puking in the
bathtub at a stranger's house, only to drive home drunk

it was getting high in taco bell parking lots and more beer
and truckloads of racist rednecks hurling slurs at 60 miles an hour

it was following trucks to their own party, on the wrong side of
town, crashing inside and cracking skulls and smashing bottles, be-
fore peeling out and letting the paranoia high seep in while red and
blue lights flashed outside of every window

It was pulling up next to a carload of white boys who flipped you
off at a red light and sticking the barrel of a shotgun outside the
window only to watch them shit their pants in slow motion before
burning rubber

It was not remembering the ride home, passing out on the lawn and
setting bad examples for younger brothers and then waking up to
discover the phone number you got last night at the party belongs to
a married woman who's husband happens to be in prison

That was the 90s.

21 years ago

Twenty-one years ago
I was talking about this other day
People say,
"1992...wow, what a long time ago!"
And it was.
But not really.

Lots of folks condemn this event and what went down, but not me.
It was necessary.
It was required.
It was lady "justice" tied down in a chair
and forced to watch the aftermath of her so-called blindness.
The fear then was palpable.

Hunter Thompson writes about striking sparks anywhere
in the 60s
shit, in the 90's everything was doused in gasoline and napalm You
could feel the heat from coast to coast
and for a little while
oh, such a small while in retrospect
people actually listened!
The nation took notice and said: goddamn!
These people are serious
and the pigs and the politicians actually *tried*
to clean up their act there for little while
the propaganda re: the "new" LAPD
was a direct result of this historic event

Why?
Because actions always speak louder than words

I say this in reference to then
and also to now
where little has changed or become worse

And we must remember that that energy is always there, bubbling
just under the surface
but we have learned how to forget it

We have traded our anger for convenience
our sense of justice for "smart" phones

But it's there
the rage is always there
anger is a gift, after all
and it always will be

circles

Two different circles
from two lifetimes ago,
intersected one day
in death
leaving me speechless
not because of the shock
but because there was no one left
to talk to about them
The circles keep getting smaller
All the technology in the world
and still thousands of miles
separate me from the past
yet it still finds me
Sometimes I wish I didn't run away
I relate now to vets who saw combat
And can only talk to certain people
about what they saw
no one else comes close
It's either that or go nuts
And on a long enough timeline
I suspect we all lose it,
to one degree or another

phone calls from ghosts

That's Not Who I am Anymore

It's late Saturday night and the phone rings. It's been a long day and the ice cold root beer chilling in the freezer box will have to wait. Your mind is nowhere at the moment except maybe to get rid of the obvious wrong number caller and get back to task at hand - unwinding.

Except when you pick up the phone, the voice on the other end of the line is vaguely familiar and they know your name. Unwinding shifts into uncoiling and finally unraveling. After a few mundane pleasantries you discover exactly who the voice is and the conversation slinks down the drain from there. You want to hang up except for one little detail:

"I'm dying..." they say.

And the only thing on your mind at that exact moment is that it is much better to let unknown phone numbers go to voicemail than it ever is to answer them.
Remember this.

How does one even reconcile someone saying that? Much less, over the phone and from an era you don't live in anymore? Further still, from someone who burned you years ago and whom you had written off for already dead..?

The answer is simple. You don't.

Sometimes ghosts from the past reach out from beyond the pages you have written them into and try to drag you back to Hell. But I am no longer one of the damned.

I did my penance. I walked through the valley of the shadow of death and wrote my sins in blood, thus, redemption was granted.

The funniest thing of all (to me) is that I granted it to myself. No God required. I peeked behind the curtain and found only my own reflection there.

And yet it's not even all that grandiose or dramatic. In fact, it's quite the opposite. That's not who I am anymore!

I've talked many times over the years about the bonds that emergency services people develop with one another - cops can only talk to other cops, EMS to EMS, nurses to other nurses and so on. And that bond seems unbreakable...until you realize that what gives it its strength is the job by itself, nothing more. Once you leave the circle that bond is weakened and often times, destroyed.

It's hard to explain - you don't come home and talk to your significant other about the heinous shit you went through - they'd never understand. They might listen but they could never hear you. It's important to be understood when you go through these kinds of things.

Retired paramedics don't talk to medics still on the job. Why? There's nothing to talk about.

I realize this is all abstract, especially considering the pretense of terminal illness delivered by strangers in the night, but to put it another way: you harbor (and eat, swallow) a lot of dark shit in these professions and you must expel it in one way or another.

That's it. It's not a choice. If you do not, it eats away at you like a cancer.

No one drifts into any of these jobs and walks away unscathed. Everyone copes. Everyone loses a piece of their own humanity. Some use booze, drugs, smokes, dope, violence, self-pity, rage, food, sex, abuse - some of them use all of these things. And then some use art.

I chose art.

And for my sins, I wrote them all down and put them into books - two to be exact. Some of you have read some of these things, some of them I keep to myself.

That's the discipline.

Recently, during a question and answer session in Tucson, someone said to me:

I bet if you had never done EMS, you would have never wrote that book.

I scoffed at that. I thought about it for a minute and told the person that I was a writer before I ever even thought about EMS. True, the books might not have been as dark but they still would have 'been'.

Then again, I have always let the darkness leak from my mind down onto the page because it has always been with me in one form or another. EMS merely opened up another chasm, one which I flourished in and ultimately burned to the ground.

So then what of the phone call?

Well, nothing.

I listened, for nearly an hour, to a man I once knew pour his guts out, lamenting for burning bridges and torching himself in the process. He wanted to apologize and clutch at straws that don't exist anymore. He wanted me to know that he was dying.

It might seem odd but I have no reaction to these kinds of things because I excised all of it from my core a long time ago. I am not the same person I was then.

I am no longer 'in the shit' looking for the next high and scraping asphalt at 135 mph with the sounds of death screaming past my ears as the lights and sirens blare at 3 a.m.. I am no longer in the brotherhood of blood and fire.

I never belonged there to begin with and ultimately found my way back to who I really am. What was I ever doing there to begin with other than proving to myself that I could? Chalk it up to research - life experience - whatever. Chalk it up to the past.
It birthed two books. I'm good with that because that world is dead

to me and has been that way for a long time now.

My priorities have changed - I have changed. So when someone calls you from the past and you answer the phone in the present, the news tends to be full of static...among other things,

I have always been able to close the door on the past without ever looking back, especially when the experience was negative.

Burn me? I won't just bury you, I will cremate you so that you don't just become a distant memory, you will become forgotten altogether. Ashes to ashes.

I am not a heartless bastard.

But I am a man of my word.

I am who I always have been.

A rattlesnake may shed its skin but it is still a rattlesnake.

I have no pity to give.

I have no empathy

nor sympathy.

What I do have is acknowledgement.

I also have a book of matches

and a family canister of gasoline.

Fwoosh.

mind's eye

I read somewhere once that if you stare at a person
for about six seconds or more,
it usually means that you either want to fuck that person
or kill them

You could argue that's the same thing
and get absolutely no argument from me

After all, we all die a little on the inside during these kinds of ex-
changes

In the movies, this is an unspoken rule behind bars
Fuck or fight, fight or flight

But the story always ends the same way

And people love to talk about the uncomfortable silences
all the time,
as if they have any inclination
as to what they really mean
But everything you ever wanted to know
but were afraid to ask
is in the eyes

Windows to the soul,
maybe
but more likely peepholes
to an exchange of bodily fluids,
in one way or another

We die 1,000 times
in our minds
and conquer hearts 1,000 more
And no one bats an eyelash

latchkey kids and jehovah's amazing technicolor dream park

I was a latchkey kid
After school, my younger brother and I would be at home
by ourselves for a few hours
before our mom made it home from work
Needless to say we got into a lot of trouble
but one day some polite White kids came to the door
with a book that looked like Jesus
sharing a plate of chicken wings
with gleeful children and docile,
smiling lions in paradise

The kids that came to the door were dressed in white
dress shirts, slacks and skinny ties
they were friendly
They wanted me to read their book
and they said they would be back
the next day
to talk to me about it.
Simple enough
So what did I do?
I read the book

Even at the age of 12 this kind of stuff made me laugh
I read their book alright,
cover-to- cover
paying particular attention to the pictures of people
playing with lions and tigers and sharks
and giant black widow spiders
I also noted the absence of anyone
that looked like myself
or my brother

All of this stuff was in stark contrast to my
Mötley Crüe records and Iron Maiden posters
and the pentagrams on my walls
I was a heavy metal kid
I had long hair, played guitar in a rock band

and wore ripped jeans and a jean jacket with patches on it

During those years, the religious fundies
tried to vilify the music I loved
I remember being invited to Christian pizza parties
where parents would show religious propaganda films
showing the "dangers" of heavy metal music
evolution and science
all the while enticing the kids
with soda, candy and pizza
The Jehovah kids came back the next day
and to my surprise
they wanted money for the book!
Again, I laughed
this time in their face.
I gave them their book back
They never came back but this kicked off
a series of attempts to convert me
into believing that lambs, lions and White people
existed in some suburban park in the sky
surrounded by rainbows, water, food
and marvels of modern construction

As I grew older
the logical fallacies of this scenario multiplied
I would ask the book peddlers more and more questions
They never had any answers
Where is this place, exactly?
Where does that food come from?
Are you still slaughtering the animals
that you're cuddling up next to in the picture?
That looks like concrete
are there concrete mixers in paradise?
Who lays the concrete?
Let me guess, Mexicans
Who cuts the grass? (See above)
Why is everyone White?
Where is the rainbow coming from?
Why is there water
if Paradise is in the clouds

wouldn't there need to be clouds above them
in order for water and rainbows to exist?
Why is everyone dressed in white?
Who built the structure they're using?
Where do the building materials come from?
Are the trees providing oxygen?
Are the people providing carbon dioxide?
Really?
In Paradise?
Where does everyone shit and piss?
Is there plumbing in Paradise?
Where does the sewage go?
Hell?

These kinds of questions continued
to not only make me laugh
but also to make me think critically
about what was thrown my way about western concepts
of the afterlife
I ended up studying afterlife concepts
in both eastern and western societies
and yes, I read the bible in its entirety
The magician, Penn Jillette, said
most people who read the bible from cover to cover
end up atheists
I can attest to this
because it happened to me
One of my favorite comedians, David Cross
talks about reading the bible when he was younger and saying,
"People actually believe this shit?!"
That was my reaction exactly

I am biased however my criticism
these days goes beyond western religion
I am opposed to eastern fundies as well
which places me right where I was at age 12
laughing my ass off at lions and White people
sharing chicken wings in a park
that's probably tended to
by Mexicans on a cloud

the best years of your life!

"These are the best years of your life!"

They sold us that line in high school
Sold, is actually too kind,
they lined us up like a firing squad
and shot us in the face
at 50 yards
with promises of horseshit and rainbows
Most swallowed

I remember it well.
In fact, I remember sitting there
while the mannequin drill Sergeant standing before everyone
spewed forth its bile and shrieked:

"Thesssee are the besssst yeeearrrssss of your lifeeeeeeeee...ssssol-
dierrr..."

I sat there and pulled the imaginary pistol
from the back of my jeans
and pointed it to my temple.
I looked at the mannequin and said:

"If that's true, I am going to kill myself."

And so I did

I squeezed the trigger
and blew my high school mind
all over the classroom
Standardized bits of test material
splattered against the walls and scattered
raining down upon SAT scores and letter jackets

I murdered my high school self,
right there, in senior history class
while everyone else signed year books
My body slumped over and fell to the tile

my classmates went about their business
and no one noticed me bleeding out on the floor
No one mourned my loss
Not even me
That was my ticket out of there
I never looked back,
though the ghosts of that era still write me letters
from time to time
I never answer them
I too am a ghost

the joneses

Once, I gave a dead man a ride
to the morgue downtown
He died at home, peacefully
in his bed
and his family ordered us up
like room service
and in we went
on Any Street, Suburban USA
and took a dead and rigor man
from his bed for a ride
He was naked, clammy
eyes wide open
and stiff as a board
we covered him with a sheet
and never said a word to his family
it was like moving furniture
The ride itself was uneventful
neither of us rode in the back with him
but I'd be lying if I said I did not peek
in the rear view mirror a few times
just to see if our guest sat up suddenly
He didn't
because he was a stiff
the hospital insisted that we
wheel him in through the back door
where the deliver food and other supplies
so here we are
two guys, bringing in a corpse
as if he were so much bread
the other delivery guys looked at us like we were nuts
and maybe we were
The morgue itself was cold
Silent
and filled with bodies
which sat on stainless steel tables
which had depth to them
in order to collect bodily fluids
the man who signed for the body

was black as pitch with red eyes
he said nothing
and we left the man there
among his own
and walked back out through the delivery door
to rush to another call
of the dying, but not yet dead
Me, an atheist
a former journalist
wondering about the death rituals
of people in suburban USA
and how keeping up with the Joneses
means calling up a couple of men
in white shirts
to take your dead father for a ride
downtown
to the morgue
for storage
on a hot summer day
when you have nothing left
but to send off your loved ones
like so much rubbish

one day you're raising hell

1

What a trip
this'll make sense to absolutely no one
but then, this really isn't the medium
for that kinda thing anyway
god, I hate the internet sometimes
This is a face to face conversation at best
for the homies no longer here
the ones you shed blood, mud and 40s with
None of you are in that circle
or from that time
But I dunno where else to pour my head out
or this beer
except on this paper here
for strangers
Things sure are weird
The fuck am I gonna do?
post this on Fakebook and wait
for a bunch of snarky and dickish comments?
No thanks
It's like a disconnect in time
or maybe this is what they mean by a rift in time
when two worlds that have been disconnected
for decades
are loosely reconnected by a few key strokes
and junior detective work
Probably not though
obituaries do this sometimes
Goddamnit
Certain things I can remember like yesterday
and they really do seem like yesterday, man
or least not that long ago but holy fuck
when you actually look down?
You realize how far into the deep water you have waded

Goddamn the internet and the ease of looking things up
and reliving the past
Idle hands and all that jazz
these here Devil's tools
Some things are best left undisturbed
In my mind, I'm young again
cruising the boulevard
and looking for trouble
sharing beers and frajos and taking cues
from the older homies
like my homeboy's older brother
(who's dead now)
and learning how to be down
I'm in love again
with life, with death
with a different hyna each night
I throw up the set and walk on fire
slowly,
as I drift into another dimension
vatos locos forever, aye

Or maybe not
Maybe that was just a movie
maybe memories are better than reality
goddamn how time changes things
one day you're raising Hell
and the next
you are trembling
at the mention of it

errand boys and grocery clerks

I feel like Colonel Kurtz again
holed up in a prison of my own making
with the polished skulls of the dead surrounding me
their vacant eye sockets accusing me
taunting me
cursing me

They wanted me dead for what they called 'treason'
I've felt like Kurtz before
a long time ago
and so I ran
as far as I could go
long until I reached the water
at the edge of the world
the voices stopped
All of them except for my own

A night with no moon
the sound of waves crashing
in the distance
I could feel the water pool
beneath my feet
slip away
slowly making the sand beneath me soft
beckoning it to swallow me whole
And so it did
burying me up to my neck
I am paralyzed and burned by the sunlight
eaten alive by crabs and birds
Here I remain
screaming for any and all to listen
to my story
alas no one hears in this place
so I wait for the tide
to pull me out to sea
forever

tradition

You want to know what traditions we have in my family?
Let me tell you
We have this great tradition of not speaking
It can go on forever
The first one to contact the other is a pussy
Simple enough, yea?
It's great
I can go years without speaking a single word to someone
In their mind, it's my fault and vice-versa
No one calls anyone and no one ever admits that they are wrong
That shit is for pussies and faggots
We all sit around and curse each other
while we wait for the phone to ring
My grandfather was fantastic at this tradition
He was so good at it that he managed to go to his grave
without saying more than twenty words to me his whole life
He was definitely not a pussy!
Of course I think I should get an honorary mention
for never reaching out to him for my entire life
I made a promise a long time ago
that I would not attend his funeral
I kept that promise
That tough old mother fucker went to the grave
without knowing his firstborn son's children
Many of us are doing the same thing
Why?
Because that's fuckin' tradition

acoma street

1

The alleyway behind the house where I grew up
was nothing special
It was home to bums pushing trash carts
and urinating on the walls in the alley
behind the house,
the occasional assault
blood-stained concrete and gutter rot
 It has not changed in the years since I called it my playground
nor since the years when I returned
only to discover that things are smaller than you remember
and not quite as bright

2

The house that I grew up in is smack dab in the middle
of an industrial wasteland
without a future
unless you call the sweeping gentrification progress
I do not
I have looked at the old neighborhood
through internet eyes and marveled
as those who long for "home" often do
how unchanged it is
in a city that has done nothing but
I have so many memories in that house
they range from the whimsical
to the criminal
I used to steal penny candy at the 7-11
behind the alley when I was a kid
That lasted until my friend was arrested
for stealing exactly four chocolate footballs
and a packet of gum
How that is justice I will never know
that cop must have been a real dickhead
but at least he didn't kill him
How times change

3

There was a thrift store at the other end of the alley
We used to call it El Segunda
I used to dig through the trash compactor
for toys
I found a stamp collection there once
I still have it
It's amazing to me that through everything
I have held onto
or let go of
through the years
the stamp collection remains

4

The hard luck alley behind my house
home to fuckups, winos and more
was no stranger to trouble
It was there, one day
in my hood, on my block
that a man in a red pick-up truck
stopped next to where we were playing
opened his door and offered to me
a brand new leather jacket,
which he patted with his hand
if only I would climb inside
I was six
I remember the pit in my stomach
and telling him to 'go to hell!'
then booking my ass home to tell my parents
that a man tried to take me
My father, pistol in tow
looked for that sonovabitch for a long time
but never found him
other kids of that era were not so lucky
and I do not think I would be here today
writing this to you
had I climbed into that truck

We used to make the kids fight each other
in the front yard
my brother, my cousins
against the neighborhood kids
we would bet on them
one toddler against another
as they tried to beat the shit out of one other
until they started crying, faces bloody, mocos running
while we cheered and laughed
barbecued and drank beer
These days that would have been newsworthy
viral even
in the old days it was simply how it was
so many things were
with no one to look over your shoulder
with a camera, broadcasting to strangers
inviting all the moral judgements
of those who pretend their households
ain't made of glass

6

My diet, at least the things that I can remember
consisted of fried bologna
fried Spam
with mustard
scrambled egg sandwiches
with ketchup
cereal with either water or orange juice
as a substitution for milk
because I am lactose intolerant
and lots of Ramen noodles with butter,
no soup
I was a skinny, pasty kid with a bowl-shaped haircut
a chip on my shoulder
and a pit in my stomach
that I still contend with today
After getting my ass kicked a few times

I took my father's words about defending myself
a little too seriously
and beat a kid at school one day,
even kicked him in the face
when he was crumpled up on the playground
I do not remember why
These days that would have been newsworthy
in the old days it was simply how it was
so many things were that way
now, people make an example
out of you for your sins
and you are crucified online
for starters

7

I grew up with a White kid named Brian
who was my friend
he lived across Broadway
on the proverbial other side of the tracks
which may as well have been in another universe
Brian was afraid of Black people
which was something I could not understand
back then
one day
I introduced him to my friend Sam,
Who lived across the street
in a tiny shack by the railroad tracks
once in a while
Sam would take me for hamburgers
in his Cadillac
I can still smell the cigar smoke
that would envelop his frame
wherever he went
once, when I introduced Brian to Sam
he ran all the way home
back across the road
to the comfort of his familiar surroundings
where Blacks never dared
We grew apart and went separate ways

but I saw Brian, years later
in high school of all places
my hair was long
and I was alone, angry
a stranger in a strange land
looking for a sign
Brian appeared
and he was still afraid of Black people
we never spoke again

8

Years later, during college
I moved back to the neighborhood
Back to what felt like home at the time
I moved back into the house
of my childhood
no longer a child
and with ill intentions
with my best friend
The refrigerator held a small stash
of microwave burritos
bologna, beer and moldy bread
The dishes in the sink overflowed
with murky water
and crusted plates
We'd sit around all day getting high,
Drunk and then high again
while the gangster neighbors came over
talked about the hood
and asked to borrow my grandfather's gun

My homeboy almost died one night
after his mom brought him a milkshake
and a meal
Turns out he was lactose intolerant too
but he had no idea how severe
until that night
after his mom left, he started to get sick
and couldn't breathe

This Is Fine

I watched as he lurched about the house
the front porch
and threw up everywhere
struggling to breathe
By that time, my car wasn't running anymore
and neither of us had health insurance
or cash
nor did we feel entitled to either
such things weren't high on the priority list back then
I hesitated on calling an ambulance or the cops
because for one,
the cops never helped anyone in my neighborhood
and two
we didn't have any money
So I called his mom
While she was on her way to take him to the hospital
I asked my friend if there was anything I could do
but there wasn't
For some reason, I laughed hysterically
while he came very near death
I couldn't stop laughing
I don't know if it was nerves
or if I am just a sadist
but I felt bad ever since
He'll never forgive me for that
Another time, we were driving along Broadway
right by the Segunda
in my carrucha
a nasty, sticker-covered green Subaru with 4WD
I don't remember if I was drunk but I made a left turn
when I shouldn't have
some lady
also in a Subaru
smashed into my car
on the passenger side
When I got out and saw that her car
was all fucked up
I laughed my ass off
in the middle of Broadway
on a sunny Denver afternoon

way back before the weed flowed free
and the white flocks flocked
to buy up all the land
She didn't think it was very funny
Neither did my insurance company

9

One time we stayed up all night
getting high and watching porno
which, back then
meant tapes from some godawful little store
once the sun came up
and we were high enough
we caught the bus to church
to "find god"
It never happened
We ended up in a church
where the only language spoken was Spanish
and played musical chairs
standing and kneeling and standing again
with bloodshot eyes
and shit-eating grins
after service we caught the bus to another church
(a white one)
and got suckered into joining a bible study class
That lasted all of half an hour
before we left in search of more weed
and a way home

10

There were so many crazy things that happened
in that neighborhood
things that could have landed us in jail
or dead
and I think for a long time
I was searching for my own grave
If only to stick the other foot in
the pranks we played on each other never ended

and it was considered fun to scare
the shit out of each other
with things that would shock people today
Eventually, my friend moved out
and I lived alone for a while
I remember one day in particular
it was my birthday
I was unemployed
a college dropout
and in a severe state of depression
No one called me
I had a single voicemail from a bitter ex
who reluctantly wished me happy birthday
while I started into a bottle of Jack
I remember waking up at about four
in the afternoon
to a dirty, empty house
to the realization of my own failure
and I ate a single can of corn for dinner

11

Later on, my Aunt moved in with me
and things got a little better
she kept me grounded
even though she was ungrounded
herself
she was a fuckup, like me
we saw the world through broken lenses
we got along well
it felt good to be with family then
nourishing, rejuvenating
necessary
to connect and to create those memories
of my early 20s
making up for lost time spent in suburbia
separated from them
I spent time with my cousins
aunts and uncles
sharing stories, beers and bud

in the house I grew up in
and returned to
in the concrete jungle
of an ungentrified Denver
before the city lost its identity
and I lost my own
after running away
The weekend parties
the barbecues in the park
all familia
the food, the drink
time with people no longer here
everything we take for granted on a daily basis
the freedom I felt then
is difficult to describe
but it was a good feeling
to be ignorant of a world
waiting to crush your dreams
I believe you only have a short period of time
like that in life
before you bite the apple
and learn the truth
I would give almost anything
to experience those kinds of get togethers again
those people
if only to break bread once more
to toast
to hug
to laugh
to say goodbye
God, I miss her
but she is no longer alive
cancer took her
from us
and I no longer speak
with what is left
of her broken family
Goddamn the cancer
and the chaos it creates
goddamn my memories

which seem to fade every year
For many things
they are all that I have left
of certain time periods
and certain people,
I find myself at a loss
reminiscing
when I truly had one foot in the grave
and the other in
my dreams

12

Over the course of many years
the house has seen generations
of people from my bloodline
so many people inside and out
of that house
where I grew up
many now dead and gone
It's all a blur
it strikes me with a sense of...
I don't know. Wonder?
Bewilderment
at my own children who stood outside
the same house
in awe
of how tiny it is
and at how the neighborhood looks
compared to what they take for granted
Time teaches you many things
most of all
that you can never go home again
no matter how cliché that sounds
I cherish those memories
good and bad
And goddamnit, we LIVED
I don't mean vicariously either
through some tiny window on your phone
I mean we were alive

and without the need to document every second of it
for strangers
Here's to my aunts and to my cousins
may they rest in peace
here's to my grandparents
who allowed generations of familia
to stay in that house
Here's to friends
past and present
Here's to not killing myself
and to my guardian angel
who surely must have
sighed a breath of relief when I moved
And here's to a dead city,
which lies beneath the surface of a thriving one
that no longer resembles the former,
like Tenochtitlan
all of its secrets buried and forgotten
overgrown with jungle rot
and technology
Here's to fucking up
Here's to your hometown
Here's to the street you grew up on
Here's to fucking up
Here's to Acoma Street

fear and loathing in public spaces

One of the things I loathe about being out in public
(but especially in restaurants)
is that I
without a doubt
will hear other people's conversations
This is never a good thing

It's always something bad
you know that right?
It doesn't matter who I'm with
I could be sitting at a table full of nuns and the mother fucker
behind me will be relaying a legendary tale
of bukkake and beer pong

People don't just go out and have normal conversations in public
oh no
they dredge up the most fucked up shit they can think of
for just that purpose
For whatever reason
my ears are keen to this kind of thing and it doesn't matter
what the fuck I do
I always end up listening to it

They'll talk about throwing up in the bathtub
and giving Uncle Charlie an enema
on Christmas morning
while Brenda, the waitress, pours more coffee
They'll throw in stories of the bride-to-be's
anal deflowering
over scrambled eggs smothered in ketchup
Or they'll talk about killing the prostitute in room 2309
and how "she just wouldn't go down, the bitch!"
no matter how hard he hit her with the champagne bottle
All this while the bacon wilts to the consistency of sand paper
and you're clawing the table
mustering every bit of willpower you have
not to turn around and murder everyone at the table behind you
with a fork

just so you can eat in peace
I have threatened people in restaurants
with forks before
but I digress

No one has any goddamn common decency any more
And they're loud
Jesus Christ are they loud!
You'd think you were at a bowling alley
instead of Denny's, listening to some shitbird
bellowing out laughs with spittle and gristle
over the time he got his cock stuck in the tailpipe
of his late wife's Ford
and had to call the cops
I have heard some shit, lemme tell you
It's a curse

But I think what I hate the most,
more than the discussions of someone beating their wife
or fucking the neighbor's cat,
is how often people will casually talk about racist shit
I read a post once where this guy
A Black kid
wrote about how it's only a matter of time
or alcohol
before a White person calls him "nigger"
I know this to be true because I hear all of your conversations

I've had countless meals ruined over this kind of thing
and I try - dear lord do I try -
(see the fork reference above)
not to react but it's not always so easy
Some conversations end with forks in the eye
others with guns on the sly
Bang!

You just never know who the fuck you're talking to
these days
Don't believe me?
Just listen sometime

Go on ahead and listen!
Listen to the people around you
in public spaces and tune in
to what they're talking about
I'll bet you'll be surprised
I bet you'll hear some shit that'll sour your milk

Know what you'll hear?
You'll hear the goddamn world ending,
one loud syllable at a time
And just so you know,
the world ends not with a bang but with FOX News
blaring in the background about the eeeevils of socialism
while Brenda pours more black coffee for you
as your eggs get cold
and the prostitute in room 2309 rots
while the donut patrol violates another person's rights
I know you thought it would be different
but it ain't

half-remembered dreams

The alarm clock
m|u|r|d|e|r|s
all the things we
say
resolve
comprehend
remember
hide
in our dreams
head injuries left untreated
relationships long broken
all the unspoken words
the un-had conversations
heated arguments with people
who appear again
and again
and again as
¿friends?
¡enemies!
lovers
strangers
murderers and deceivers
all of the punches never thrown
the triggers never pulled
drinks never bought
glass never shattered
bread never broken
sheets never stained
roads never traveled
all of the pain and the scars
the wounds
every goddamned stale aspiration
all of the things
that live captive
on the plantation
in your mind
they are all
dead and burned

by morning
in the waking fires
of conscious thought
without sermon
nor parting words
no requiem
they evapo r a t   e
in the midst
of hot coffee
and breaking daylight
like a page you write on
and burn at the same time

run

I run from crazy
He runs from crazy
We run from crazy

I run from crazy
He runs from crazy
We run from crazy

I run from crazy
He runs from crazy
We run from crazy

But crazy always has a way of catching up
and you cannot kill
crazy

without its stain passing through
the pores
into the bloodstream
down to the core
where pills do not reach and
psychiatrists cannot preach
and we all know how well running from yourself
works out

So run, vato
Run!

Run until the sweat pours
through open/closed
windows/doors
your mind reeling
run til the lungs burn
and then run again
until the pounding of your pulse
whispers that you are merely
running into a mirror, always
where the fear permeates the air

like so much steam in the moonlight
rising up

Run.

the grass

The grass
is always greener
on the other
side
because the assholes
over there
paint it
in hopes
that you will
hop the fence
so they can
flay you
barbecue your
carcass
and eat your soul

2017

Knowledge, knowledge, everywhere,
and all the brains did shrink;
Knowledge, knowledge, everywhere,
Nor anyone to think.

This Is Fine

www.ingramcontent.com/pod-product-compliance
Lightning Source LLC
LaVergne TN
LVHW011222080426
835509LV00005B/262